THE CROSS AND SANCTIFICATION

the Cross & Sanctification

by T.A. Hegre

BETHANY FELLOWSHIP, INC.
Minneapolis, Minnesota

Library of Congress catalog card number A-517866

Formerly Published as
THREE ASPECTS OF THE CROSS

Printed in the United States of America

To the members of Bethany Church who in the early days of my ministry so lovingly encouraged the teaching and preaching of the message of the Cross

FOREWORD

OUR roots with Ted Hegre go back about twenty years to the time when God was renewing to him the reality of the Galatians 2:20 life: "Not I but Christ liveth in me." Our contacts at that time bound us together in heart and spirit with bonds which have strengthened through the years. I remember in 1943 when he first started a "house-church" in the city of Minneapolis. How inspired I was with the eager, crowded audiences gathered there! Then they took their great launch of faith by moving to the sixty acres of land on the outskirts of the city—now the campus of the Bethany Fellowship and Missionary Training Center. Who could believe that out of nothing (no drum-beating and no wealthy supporters) would come the present buildings—dormitories, workshops, classrooms, an administration building, and an auditorium to seat twelve hundred? All this was God, believed and obeyed, the same God who said to Abraham, "Get thee out of thy country and from thy kindred. . . unto a land that I will shew thee: and I will bless thee. . . and thou shalt be a blessing."

We in the Worldwide Evangelization Crusade have the greatest respect and love for Ted Hegre and his co-workers in the Bethany Fellowship. We have good reason to, for we have had plenty of proof of the reality in them of the life of the Spirit. What Ted Hegre teaches in this book works out in life. Many more Bethany students have joined the W.E.C. than any other mission agency; indeed, Bethany is almost a W.E.C. training centre for us. Truly we can say from the evidence of twelve years that out of Bethany come men and women of God, good soldiers of Jesus Christ, the type of whom it can be said (as of the Apostle Paul) that "God has enabled them, for that He counted [them] faithful, putting them into the ministry."

In "the pursuit of God," Ted Hegre and I have followed largely the same road. We have been driven to seek the way of God "more perfectly," and to find an ever-enlarging comprehension of the breadth and length and depth and height sufficient to meet the challenges both of our personal lives and of missionary commission. With Paul, we "press toward the mark". . . , not [having] already attained either [being] already perfect," but eager to share such light as we have.

In this book Ted Hegre seeks to present a whole gospel—justification, sanctification, and enduement for service. His central theme—the threefold message of the Cross—is a basic emphasis rarely presented in this form, and so, may properly be called the special revelation given to Ted Hegre. How whole-heartedly we add our amen to this emphasis! His handling of the two-nature teaching, his differentiation between the "old man" and flesh, and his definition of flesh are illuminating. I don't cross every one of his t's (though he hopes to get me converted sometime!), and I doubt that we are meant to, for we are called to union with a glorious Person, not to a set of doctrines. Variety of insight, and even differences are really only opposite poles of infinite truth. Anything which drives us back to the written Word to find out for ourselves "whether these things [be] so" is healthy. My understanding of the crisis of sanctification and of the baptism with the Holy Ghost may be slightly different in detail but profoundly one in their being facts of the Spirit-filled life. As one of the new members of Bethany staff wrote me: "The truths brought forth in these chapters keep getting a big amen from me. Scales fell from my eyes more than once. No longer was my vision blurred, 'seeing men as trees walking,' so to speak. Muddled thinking of years began to get straightened out. From my point of view, what makes this book ring with reality is the behind-the-scenes outworking of these truths in the ordinary folk on Bethany staff, for on them is obviously the divine unction."

The Apostle Paul's declared objective was not merely to preach the Gospel and found churches but "to present every man perfect in Christ Jesus." This is the common meeting-ground of Ted Hegre, Bethany Fellowship, the Worldwide Evangelization Crusade, and many thousands of others who can be satisfied with nothing less in their lives and teaching than "the whole counsel of God." This book is in that same life stream. It will be the voice of God to many.

Norman P. Grubb
General Secretary
Worldwide Evangelization Crusade

PREFACE

THIS book contains simple studies on what is generally called the deeper life. After becoming a Christian, the writer soon discovered that in his own experience and in the experience of others whom he knew, the level of Christian living was not the same as that set forth in the Scriptures. This inconsistency caused him to seek earnestly for an answer to this perplexing problem. First he searched the books of his church and there found a recognition of the problem but no solution. Not knowing any books on the victorious life at that time, he began his own careful and prayerful search of the Scriptures. There he found the answer revealed in the deeper meaning of the Cross. First he found "the way" in his own experience; then he became aware of the doctrinal principles involved, and later learned how to explain them.

The writer taught these blessed truths in messages which we began to call "The Three Aspects of the Cross." In the early days these messages were taught with blackboard illustrations at meetings both in the home and the church. Then they appeared as articles in our bimonthly magazine, *The Message of the Cross*. Thus most of the chapters of this book have already appeared as a series of studies. Many of them also received a wide circulation in little booklets. These studies have now been revised, enlarged, and collected into this present volume. They were written years apart so that though revised, the reader may find a lack of continuity between some chapters. Perfection or excellence is not claimed—only an attempt to answer the problem of how to live a holy and fruitful Christian life.

The writer is particularly grateful to Mr. Norman P. Grubb, Director of the Worldwide Evangelization Crusade, who kindly consented to write a foreword to this volume. We are also indebted to writers in all ages. Familiarity with their writings may have resulted in quotations; however, we have not felt it necessary to secure special permission for brief quotations. Special acknowledgment and appreciation is also due to my close associates at Bethany Fellowship who have so wonderfully helped in making the publication of this book possible.

T. A. Hegre
Bethany Fellowship
Minneapolis 20, Minn.
March 2, 1960

CONTENTS

CONTENTS

CHARTS

Scripture quotations are from the
American Standard Version unless otherwise indicated

INTRODUCTORY

HAVE YOU LOST YOUR BIBLE?

"Do not my words do good to him
that walketh uprightly?" (Micah 2:7).

IF we are to rise in faith, in holy living, and in
power for service, our only true foundation is the
Word of God. Someone was once heard to pray,
"Lord, *help us believe* Thy Word." Such a prayer
we have so taken for granted that we have not noticed
the incongruity of the request. For a true Christian,
help to believe God's Word is not needed, because
believing the word of the living God should
be most easy and natural. However, the surprising
fact is that most Christians are unbelieving. Though
they trust God's Word regarding repentance and faith,
and have accepted His promise of forgiveness; though
they have received Christ and have eternal life in
Him; and though they believe in prayer (limited too
often, it is true, to making requests known)—yet
they either ignore or disbelieve most of God's great
promises for Christian victory and for power in
service.

Why, however, do Christians find it so difficult or
even impossible to believe the promises of God? Is not

a Christian a partaker of the divine nature? Does not
every Christian know and love and have vital fellowship with a personal, living God? Usually those whom
we know and love, we believe—especially those who
have a good character and reputation. Thus, to doubt
and disbelieve God is so unnatural for a believer (?)
that we can well say in the words of Scripture, "An
enemy hath done this." Mass doubt and mass unbelief are surely the works of the devil.

But *how* has the devil caused so many of us to
doubt the Word of God? Jeremiah suggested the
answer when he said, "Ye have *perverted* the words
of the living God" (Jer. 23:36). And the Psalmist
declared, "It is time for Jehovah to work; *for they
have made void thy law*" (Ps. 119:126). In question
form, the Apostle Paul states the same fact in Romans
3:31: "Do we then *make void the law*. . . ?" (A.V.).
Yes, this is exactly what has happened. God's Word
has been tampered with, "perverted," and "made void"
through the deceitfulness and trickery of the enemy
of our souls.

In speaking of the devil, Jesus said, *"The thief
cometh not, but that he may steal, and kill, and destroy"* (John 10:10). The devil begins his infamous
work by stealing. The one thing he would like to
steal from us the most is the Word of God. Thus
throughout the centuries, he has made several attempts to get rid of the Bible, to destroy it. If he had
succeeded, there would not be much hope either for
the world or the Church. Then, having failed in these
attempts to destroy the Bible, he set about to rob us
of God's Word in a subtler manner. His masterplan

took the form of "*higher criticism.*" As a result, a great number of people (several denominations, in fact) succumbed to his bold deception and *lost their Bible* as the inspired Word of God. Believing that at best the Bible "contains" the Word of God, they lost the assurance that comes by believing "thus saith the Lord." In this master-stroke, the devil destroyed faith in the major doctrines which had been believed for hundreds of years. Having then no sure foundation, such people began to magnify the word of man and found themselves ultimately to be "shifting sand" on sinking sand.

Fortunately, many in the Church did not accept these false conclusions of "higher criticism," for they *knew* that the Bible was the inspired Word of God. Then the arch-thief planned to rob even such saints of their Bible, for he introduced next a system of Bible interpretation known as "ultra-dispensationalism." Though this system was unknown for hundreds of years (during which the Church produced its best saints), nevertheless this new interpretation was advanced as a superior method of study in the Word. So here again, by dividing the Bible into various dispensational periods and applying its truths only to its particular dispensation, the enemy partially accomplished his purpose of stealing the Bible from us.

But a great number in the Church could not accept the extreme teachings of ultra-dispensationalism. Satan had these in mind also. He whose whole purpose is to steal now advanced a much more modified form of dispensationalism—a form so mild and so moderate that by the great majority of fundamentalists it was accepted. In fact, fundamentalism and *mild dispensationalism* are today almost synonymous. Yet in its tendencies, fundamentalist dispensationalism is, we believe, dangerous and mischievous, robbing us of much of the Bible, especially of the words of Christ. This system of interpretation holds that the gospel of our Lord, which He declared to be at hand, was withdrawn, and in its place a new gospel was substituted. Such teachers believe that the Church's duties are to be found only in the Epistles, and not in the Sermon on the Mount and the sayings of Christ. Their teachings imply that there are two gospels: one, the gospel of Christ, and the other, the gospel of Paul; and that for our times the gospel of Paul has the higher authority. The really dangerous sect in Corinth, they say, was the "Christ sect" who said, "I am ... of Christ" (I Cor. 1:12), and who rejected the new revelation of the doctrines of grace in Paul's letters. Such declarations as this not only "make void" the gospel of Christ, but also say believers in Christ's gospel comprised the most dangerous sect in Corinth!

Teachers of such a system have not seen the unity in God's plan of salvation, and so they teach that God has different ways of saving sinners. For instance, one of them writes, "A dispensation is defined as a period of time during which man is tested in respect to obeying some specific revelation of the will of God; seven such are found in the Bible." Then again, "Grace began with the death and resurrection of Jesus Christ; from then on, the point of testing is no longer legal obedience as a condition of salvation, but acceptance or rejection of Christ."

However, those who have not been robbed of great sections of our Bible see grace both in the Old Testament, and in the Gospels, and also in the Epistles. We believe that whether for those living in the Old Testament or New Testament times, God has had no other way of saving men except through faith in Christ and His vicarious sacrifice. Abraham was *not* saved *by law*, for the Bible says, "[Abraham] *believed* in Jehovah, and he reckoned it to him for righteousness" (Gen. 15:6). Another Scripture passage concerning the way of salvation is that classic of the Reformation, "The just shall live by faith," but this is actually found in the Old Testament (Habakkuk 2:4 A.V.). The truth is that the Old Testament period was a time of law—but not without grace; the New Testament period is a time of grace—but not without law. In both periods, *the only way of salvation has been "by grace through faith."* God has but one way of saving men.

Certainly only one generation had the privilege of seeing Christ with the physical eye; so, Old Testament saints *looked forward* spiritually to Calvary and saw Christ by faith; and today we *look back* spiritually to Calvary and "by faith alone" see Christ. However, the Holy Spirit, performing His work of revealing Christ, was present in both periods—in Old Testament times (through types, symbols, writings) and also in our times (through the complete revelation which we call the Bible).

Satan, then, as the thief, has stolen great sections of the Bible from Christians. Because of this, many Christians have lost faith in God's promises concerning holy living and power for service. For instance, we are told by some that the Sermon on the Mount is neither the Church's duty nor privilege. It is not for now. They also say that the supernatural powers enjoyed by the apostles and their followers have been withdrawn. Such powers belong only to a period of transition, and so were limited to apostolic times. In addition, they say that we are not to expect the Holy Spirit to manifest himself in the various gifts of the Spirit (as given in I Corinthians 12). "God doesn't work that way now," we are told. In *this* dispensation, righteousness of life (as seen in Matthew 5, 6, 7) and the supernatural power seen in the Book of Acts are neither possible to us nor expected of us. But if we believe these things, we have been robbed of our heritage. One reason there are so many unbelieving Christians is that teachers have unintentionally taught them to disbelieve! Instead of being exhorted to believe in God's supernatural power for Christian living and service (as well as for regeneration), we are taught that this is not God's order for today. Furthermore, if one *does* want to step out in faith, he must almost "go it alone"; he must be a pioneer, with the dead weight of an unbelieving church holding him back. Now is the very time, therefore, for those who are willing to believe God and willing to take His Word *as it is*, to refuse to let the devil steal from them any fragment of it.

If Christ has said, "He that believeth on me, the works that I do shall he do also; and greater works than these shall he do; because I go unto the Father" (John 14:12), it is up to us to believe Him and trust Him to enable us to do these "greater works." But in many Christian circles these words of Christ are also explained away by saying that the "greater works" means the saving of souls, and that soul-winning should be our emphasis. But what man can save a soul? Only God can do this! No, Jesus was not speaking about saving souls only; He was speaking about works that He did: He healed the sick, He cleansed the lepers, He cast out demons, He performed miracles. He said that we should do the same—in His power and name, of course. Now we know that healings and miracles do not save, but they make known the fact that God is in the midst of His people. Some of these "greater works," if exhibited today, would make unnecessary the expense of elaborate advertising programs that are so much in vogue in our day. Too often evangelistic campaigns are merely special meetings attended mainly by Christians. But if the Word of God were believed and preached in its fullness and in such a way that God could "confirm the word by the signs that followed" (Mark 16:20), as He did in the time of the Book of Acts, then expensive advertising and community canvasses would not be necessary to fill up the church or meeting hall. Neither would sentimental, long-drawn-out invitations be needed. In such cases every preacher with the opportunity to preach to great numbers of the lost, would hear again the cry of the congregation: "What must I do to be saved?" At present, using worldly methods, we are making little headway. Is it not time to take inventory? Is it not time to make a readjustment back to God's Word and God's methods? Have *you* lost *your* Bible?

Three Aspects of the Cross

CHRIST CRUCIFIED

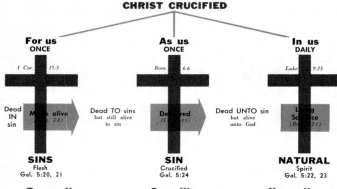

For us ONCE	**As us** ONCE	**In us** DAILY
I Cor. 15:3	Rom. 6:6	Luke 9:23
Dead IN sin — Made alive (Eph. 2:1) → Dead TO sins but still alive to sin	Delivered (Col. 3:3) → Dead UNTO sin but alive unto God	Living Sacrifice (Rom. 12:1)
SINS Flesh Gal. 5:20, 21	**SIN** Crucified Gal. 5:24	**NATURAL** Spirit Gal. 5:22, 23

Perversity
(The unregenerate man)
ONCE—a *definite* experience

"If we confess our sins, he is faithful and righteous to forgive us our sins, and to cleanse us from all unrighteousness" (I John 1:9).

"You did he make alive, when ye were dead through your trespasses and sins" (Eph. 2:1).

"Christ died for our sins" (I Cor. 15:3).

"Who his own self bare our sins in his body upon the tree, that we having died unto sins, might live unto righteousness" (I Peter 2:24).

"Thou shalt call his name Jesus; for it is he that shall save his people from their sins" (Matt. 1:21).

"Unto him that loveth us, and loosed us from our sins by his blood" (Rev. 1:5b).

"He that covereth his transgressions shall not prosper, but whoso confesseth and forsaketh them shall obtain mercy" (Prov. 28:13).

"Who was delivered up for our trespasses, and was raised for our justification" (Rom. 4:25).

Carnality
(The "old man")
ONCE—a *definite* experience

"They that are of Christ Jesus have crucified the flesh with the passions and lusts thereof" (Gal. 5:24).

"Whosoever he be of you that renounceth not all that he hath, he cannot be my disciple" (Luke 14:33).

"Knowing this that our old man was crucified with him, that the body of sin might be done away . . ." (Rom. 6:6).

"The death that he died, he died unto sin once . . . even so reckon ye also yourselves to be dead unto sin . . ." (Rom. 6:10, 11).

"One died for all, therefore all died . . . that they that live should no longer live unto themselves but unto him . . ." (II Cor. 5:14, 15).

"Ye died . . ." (Col. 3:3).

"I have been crucified with Christ; and it is no longer I that live, but Christ liveth in me" (Gal. 2:20).

"The blood of Jesus his Son cleanseth us from all sin" (I John 1:7).

"He that hath suffered in the flesh hath ceased from sin" (I Pet. 4:1).

Humanity
(The "new man")
DAILY—a *continual* application of the Cross

"If any man would come after me, let him deny himself, take up his cross **daily** and follow me" (Luke 9:23).

Discipline
"Christ also pleased not himself" (Rom. 15:3).

"I keep under my body and bring it into subjection . . ." (I Cor. 9:27).

Sacrifice
"Except a grain of wheat fall into the earth and die, it abideth alone: but if it die, it beareth much fruit" (John 12:24).

"We have this treasure in earthen vessels, that the exceeding greatness of the power may be of God and not from ourselves . . . we who live are always delivered unto death for Jesus' sake . . . death in us . . . but life in you" (II Cor. 4:7–12).

Brokenness
"The sacrifices of God are a broken spirit, a broken and a contrite heart, O God, thou wilt not despise" (Ps. 51:17).

Intercession
"This people have sinned a great sin. . . Yet now, if thou wilt forgive their sin—;" (Ex. 32:31, 32a). (See also Rom. 9:23.)

Authority
"They overcame him because of the blood of the lamb and because of the word of their testimony and they loved not their life even unto death" (Rev. 12:11).

THE THREE ASPECTS INTRODUCED

> "I [Paul] determined not to know anything among you, save Jesus Christ, and him crucified" (I Cor. 2:2).

WHAT we all need today is to know in experience the salvation to the uttermost that is ours through Christ's atoning death on the Cross. The Apostle Paul's determination when he came to Corinth was to have not only an intellectual knowledge, but also an experiential knowledge of Jesus Christ and His Cross. The initial message of the Cross, which concerns our justification before God, has been regarded as basic throughout the years and has been presented somewhat clearly. But concerning other deeper meanings of Calvary's Cross, there has been, and is, much confusion. Many have not had clear understanding of such passages of Scripture as "I die daily"; "ye have put off the old man"; "crucified with Christ"; "the old man was crucified"; "make to die the doings of the body"; "deny yourself"; "ceased from sin"; "sinneth not"; "dead unto sin"; "alive unto God," and others. For this reason, even though we are told plainly that He *always* "giveth us the victory

9

through our Lord Jesus Christ," and also that "His grace *is* sufficient for us," many Christians are still living defeated lives.

In many cases, the reason for the confusion and lack of understanding of the deeper meaning of the Cross is that there has not yet been a definite break with sin. All too many have not totally renounced self and so are still making provision for the flesh (Rom. 13:14). Until we come to an end of ourselves and make a full surrender to Christ, we shall never be able to understand the deeper truths of God's Word, for it is written, "The rich he hath sent empty away" (Luke 1:53). But on the other hand, there *are* those who really want a deeper life with God and who "hunger and thirst after righteousness." To all such, we are trusting the Lord to bring about the fulfillment of His promise, "They *shall* be filled." With these hungry souls in mind, we are setting forth in this chapter a bird's-eye view of the work of the Cross in three of its main aspects:

First, *Christ Crucified FOR Us—Our Substitute.* This aspect of the Cross of Christ deals with the unregenerate man, that is, with *perversity*—and makes possible the forgiveness of sins and regeneration.

Secondly, *Christ Crucified AS Us—Our Representative.* Here the Cross of Christ deals with the old man,* that is, with *carnality*—and makes possible both freedom from the power of sin and also the fulness of the Holy Spirit.

Thirdly, *Christ Crucified IN Us—Our Indweller.* This aspect of the Cross of Christ does not deal with

---

* For explanation of the term, *the old man*, as used in this book, see chapters 3 and 4.

sin but with humanity (or the physical man). It deals with the new man. The daily Cross is for disciplined control of the physical body, the sacrifice of the body that others too may live, intercessory prayer, and victorious warfare against Satan.(We shall discuss each of these in separate chapters later.)

Though all who have been exposed to the Scriptures have some conception of the Cross and its meaning, yet even the most enlightened see only in part. Our capacity to see the whole truth of God's so great a salvation is very limited at best. The simple story of the four blind men and the elephant seems applicable here. One of the blind men felt the elephant's leg and said, "I *know* that an elephant is like a tree"; another, feeling his ear, *knew* that an elephant was like a fan; a third felt his side and *knew* an elephant was like a rough wall; still another felt his tail and said, "I certainly can't see how you all can be so mistaken, for any one would *know* that an elephant is like a rope." All saw the elephant—in part. Did any really see the elephant?

In the salvation of our souls, God has provided so much that even if we see in Calvary all that Luther saw, together with all that Calvin saw, and in addition all that Wesley saw, we still would not know the whole of God's tremendous work on our behalf at Calvary. The liberals see and accept only the third aspect of the Cross—a form of self-denial. Some fundamentalists (there are several varieties of those who believe the Bible is the Word of God) generally see only the first aspect. Holiness people see the first and second aspects but as a rule not the third. Others, accepting only the first and third aspects, would not consider the second crisis at all. Then, is not what we all need a revelation of the *full* meaning of the Cross? We must each appropriate *all* the benefits of Calvary. To this end may the Lord himself enlighten us now as we look into the three aspects in greater detail.

The first aspect of the Cross, *Christ Crucified FOR Us—Our Substitute,* deals with unregenerate man, the man "dead in trespasses and sins." First, the Holy Spirit begins to convict a man of his sins and to reveal to him that he is lost, outside the fellowship of God, and subject to eternal death. As this sinner responds and confesses his sins, the Holy Spirit through the Word shows clearly that the stroke due him fell on Christ (Isa. 53:8, margin). "Christ *died* for our sins" (I Cor. 15:3), and "His own self *bare* our sins in his body upon the tree, that we, having died unto sins, might live unto righteousness" (I Peter 2:24). In this first work of the Cross, the Holy Spirit points out to the sinner the only way of salvation from sins. He reveals that God's plan is to save His people *from* —not *in*—their sins. God's terms for our receiving His provision of salvation are twofold: "repentance toward God, and faith toward our Lord Jesus Christ" (Acts 20:21; faith is turning *from* sin; faith is turning *to,* and receiving Christ as Lord and Saviour. Only when the sinner repents and trusts, does God forgive and regenerate. Therefore the sinner *must* repent, *must* forsake his sins, and *must* believe that Christ died for his sins. "Confess your sins," says I John 1:9. That is our side of it, and if we do our part and receive Jesus Christ as our personal Lord and Saviour, God will do His part, applying the benefit and value of the Cross. He will both forgive us and regenerate us, for "He is *faithful* and *righteous* to forgive us our sins." Thus we will be "born again," and it will be true of us as it is declared in Ephesians 2:1, "You did he *make alive,* when ye were dead through your trespasses and sins." Salvation, then, is not by believing a doctrine or confessing a creed, but salvation is by becoming united to a Person, and that Person is Jesus Christ.

But is forgiveness and regeneration *all* that the Cross can do for us? No, it is neither all that our God can nor wants to do. He meets the sinner's first need and perhaps his *only* need at that time as he sees it—namely, salvation from the guilt and penalty of sin. But this is just the beginning of God's work. Very soon the young convert, now no longer spiritually dead but alive unto God, knows that he needs a deeper work of grace in his heart. He knows that he has other needs besides the forgiveness of sins. Though forgiven, he is not always victorious, for there seems to be a *power of sin* in his life so that he "may *not* do the things that [he] would" (Gal. 5:17). He loves the Lord and His will, yet he finds himself in bondage so that he can *not* obey the Lord perfectly. Nor does he have abiding joy. Within is a conflict, for "the flesh lusteth against the Spirit, and the Spirit against the flesh" (Gal. 5:17). To be sure, at times he has joy, but very much of his experience is up and down. The great tragedy in the Christian Church is that many are told this is the normal Christian experience, and so lose heart and go back to the world.

It is just here that the Holy Spirit can reveal to the hungry a deeper aspect of the Cross: *Christ Crucified AS Us—Our Representative*. This aspect deals not with Christ taking upon himself the stroke which was our due, but with Christ *bearing us to the Cross*. To the soul that really hungers and thirsts for righteousness and seeks for a way out, God reveals that Jesus died *as* us: "One died for all, therefore *all died;* . . . that they that live should no longer live unto themselves, but unto him" (II Cor. 5:14, 15). God's Word also says that "our old man *was* crucified with him" (Rom. 6:6).

God's Word declares specifically, "He [Christ] died for all." But it also says, "Therefore all died." Both statements must be accepted and believed. To receive salvation we must accept God's terms, which are repentance and faith—faith in the fact of Christ's death *for us* as our Substitute on Calvary's Cross. It is exactly the same regarding the second aspect of the Cross. Though Christ's death *as* us happened almost two thousand years ago, in our experience this becomes real only when we meet Christ's terms. What are these terms? Surrender and faith. "If any man would come after me, let him deny himself" (Matt. 16:24). Surrender is the denial of self—not the denial of things, and not even self-denial (so-called). Denial of self is an utter unconditional surrender to Jesus Christ, including the giving up of all my "rights to myself." Here is the root of sin in experience—my idea that I have a right to myself, or that *these are my rights*. Thus, the reason that we are so easily irritated, jealous, touchy, impatient, anxious, proud, or angry (to say nothing of other gross sins) is that we have not denied ourselves. Our part is to deny self, to nail the disposition to have our own way to the Cross. The Word says that positionally "our old man *was* crucified with him." It is already done, for there we *were* crucified; there we *died;* there we *were* buried. As far as God is concerned, He is through with the old man. However, in our experience, God will not make this real until we give Him permission by making an absolute surrender to Him—a surrender so complete that death (to self) is the only word that can properly describe it. Then we can go on and reckon ourselves "dead unto sin, but alive unto God in Christ Jesus" (Rom. 6:11).

And so, God's part in redemption through the person of Jesus Christ is already full and complete. Our part is to get rightly adjusted to what Jesus Christ *has* already *done*—our part is to come and take *all* that He has provided. Many come and take only the forgiveness of sins; some come and take a little deeper measure of victory; but God wants us to have *the full value of the death of Christ.* God's table is spread, and "all things are now ready." His great invitation is "Come" (Luke 14:17), for "according to your faith be it done unto you" (Matt. 9:29). As we mentioned before, the principles involved in "entering in" to Christ crucified *as* us are the same as in Christ crucified *for* us. If we will but deny ourselves and forsake all that we have, giving ourselves with full abandonment to God, He will by the Holy Spirit make the Cross real in our experience. Then we will find that we are not only dead to *sins* (plural)—this *must* be our attitude if we are Christians at all—but we will also be able to "reckon ourselves dead to *sin*" (singular). Literally, we will be *delivered "out of* the power of darkness, and *translated . . . into* the kingdom of the Son of his love" (Col. 1:13). This truth, positionally true of all, will become experientially true, so that we will have a right to say no to temptation. We will have a right also to say no to the devil and to the claims of the old life. "If the Son shall make [us] free, [we] shall be free indeed."

Now there are many that think this second aspect of the Cross is a daily dying. But the context very plainly tells us that it is a definite crisis experience, for Romans 6:10, 11 says Christ "died unto sin *once*: . . . Even so reckon ye also yourselves to be dead unto sin." This must be a *crisis experience*, a definite break with sin, a definite break with bondage to the flesh. If this is still a daily experience with us, it must be because we have not utterly denied self, we have not renounced all that we have, and we are still making provision somewhere for the flesh. God's Word says, "Make *not* provision for the flesh, to fulfil the lusts thereof" (Rom. 13:14).

Here, then, in this second aspect of the Cross of Christ, is God's provision for the old man, for carnality—namely, *death*. There must be a willingness to die to the old life and all that pertains to it, and then a trusting the Holy Spirit to make real in us what God's Word promises. God's provision is to *"put away*, as concerning your former manner of life, the old man, that waxeth corrupt after the lusts of deceit; . . . and *put on* the new man, that after God hath been created in righteousness and holiness of truth" (Eph. 4:22–24).

Finally, there is still a deeper meaning of the Cross of Christ, a third aspect: *Christ Crucified IN Us— Our Indweller*, which deals with the physical man, or *humanity*. It is here we have a daily application of the Cross. Jesus said unto them all, "If any man would come after me, let him deny himself, and *take up his cross daily*, and follow me" (Luke 9:23). This deeper experience is not a daily dying to sin, but a daily bearing of the cross, and is necessary (as we show in separate chapters later) for several reasons: for the control of the body; for sacrificial living; for a spirit of brokenness; for intercession for others; and for warfare against Satan and spiritual hosts of wickedness.

First, we shall very briefly consider the control or discipline of the body. Though the *old* man (which was in bondage to the devil and the world) has been crucified, yet the *new* man needs to be brought into full subjection to God. Even though we have been forgiven our sins, and also have been cleansed from *all* sin, there must be right living and growth, and full adjustment to God and His purpose. Genuine though the blessing of sanctification may have been, it is not a state of grace from which we can *not* fall. It may be lost. It is necessary therefore to live a disciplined life—"to keep under the body and bring it into subjection" (I Cor. 9:27 A.V.).

In the old life, the body was an instrument of sin and under the dominion of the old man (which was energized by the devil); the body itself was not sin but was an instrument of sin; the body was not bad, but was simply under the wrong management.

But as we have seen, that old management can come to an end. Through the wondrous working of the Cross, in place of the wrong disposition (the old man), God gives us the disposition of Christ. Therefore we are admonished, "Neither present your members unto sin as instruments of unrighteousness; but *present yourselves unto God,* as alive from the dead, and your members as instruments of righteousness unto God" (Rom. 6:13). The body has appetites, desires, urges, and passions which are not wrong in themselves; but if these are not controlled by the Holy Spirit, they will become wrong. For this reason we must keep the body under the control of Christ and bear the *daily* cross.

Christ himself had to bear a *daily* cross to keep His body under the control of the Holy Spirit. We are told concerning Him that "Christ also pleased not himself" (Rom. 15:3). He did not have a sinful nature, yet He had to stay under the discipline of the Holy Spirit. He lived only to please God. His daily cross was not always seen, but it was a cross nevertheless. For instance, as He was tempted of the devil in the wilderness, He fasted for forty days and then became hungry. Under ordinary circumstances would it have been wrong to eat? No. But Christ did not eat, for this suggestion to eat was a temptation from the devil, and therefore to yield would have been sin. So, even though Christ's body demanded food, He pleased not himself but chose to trust the Father to feed Him whenever His Father's purpose in the wilderness had been fulfilled.

To sum up this working of the Cross in the control of the body, we will use again two simple illustrations. First, our eating. It is not wrong to eat, but it can become wrong if we eat too much or too often. Just here we need the continual application of the Cross to keep our body under control. Second, our sleeping. Of course sleep is not wrong; it is necessary. But we know sleep can become wrong if we sleep when God wants us to be awake. Lest our bodies become again the instruments of sin, we must bear our cross and not please ourselves. Moreover, every other appetite and desire of the body—even though the appetite is not wrong in itself—must be kept under the control of the Holy Spirit.

Great confusion exists right here. So many locate sin in the body, thinking that sin is something material, that it is a sort of "lump of something" that either must be removed by some kind of spiritual surgery, or that must be retained as long as we are in the body. But sin is not material and does not have its seat in the body. Sin, rather, is in the soul, in the spiritual part of man. Sin is a tendency, an attitude, a wrong way of looking at things. Sin stems from *self* being at the center of the life. But when we surrender fully to Christ and trust Him to forgive and also to cleanse us from all unrighteousness (through the Cross), then sin is removed and the taint gone. The heart that is pure and filled with perfect love is ready for the anointing with the Holy Spirit. But even then, lest we again begin to please ourselves, we need the daily application of the Cross to maintain the decision made in the crisis of sanctification.

Yes, we need the daily outworking of the Cross not only in disciplining the body but also in sacrificing the body. That others may live, we must be willing to sacrifice all, even life itself. This is what the Apostle Paul means in I Corinthians 15:31 where he says, "I die daily." The context is very plain and shows clearly that the reference is to physical death. This is not speaking about sin; this is speaking about Paul's physical body. Daily he was willing to hazard his life to death. The preceding verse says, "We also stand in jeopardy every hour" (I Cor. 15:30), while the following verse declares, "After the manner of men I fought with beasts at Ephesus" (I Cor. 15:32). To apply this passage to "death to sin" would require the greatest stretch of imagination and the greatest liberty in exegesis. Here Paul does not refer to sin at all, but to his willingness to sacrifice his life that others may live. We have this truth further explained in II Corinthians 4:7–12: "We have this treasure in earthen vessels, that the exceeding greatness of the power may be of God, and not from ourselves; . . . For we who live are always *delivered unto death* for Jesus' sake, . . . So then *death* worketh in us, but life in you." Thus, not only must our body be kept under control (so that it does not rule us but we rule it), but also this disciplined body of ours must be used for others. In order that others may live, we must be "broken bread and poured out wine."

In Romans 12:1 we are exhorted to present our bodies as a living sacrifice to God—"holy and acceptable." But man in his natural state is *not* holy; he is *not* acceptable. Controlled by the old man, the body is neither holy nor acceptable. Only the man who has experienced the crucifixion of this old life (the second aspect of the Cross) *can* present himself to God as a living sacrifice. Thus this third aspect of the Cross goes on to deal not with sin but with the physical body (or humanity), that our bodies may be kept under control and sacrificed so that others may live.

This is the secret of fruit bearing which the Bible and all nature tells about: "Except a grain of wheat fall into the earth and die, it abideth by itself alone; but *if it die*, it beareth much fruit" (John 12:24). This verse does not refer to surrendering the old man (self-life) to God, for we do not plant bad seed but good. This verse refers to handing over the new life to God to plant it so that thereby it may bring forth fruit. In order to make bread for others, God will break the one who has *already* been cleansed from sin, and has *already* been liberated from the domination of self, the world, and Satan.

There is another application of this third aspect of the Cross—intercessory prayer. This, too, has nothing to do with sin, but rather with the outworking of the purpose of God in the new man. Intercessory prayer is not mere praying *for* someone. It is "the supplication of a righteous man [that] availeth much in its working" (James 5:17). Moses broke out in a great sob as he prayed for his people who had exchanged their Deliverer and Supplier of every need for a golden calf. This was no ordinary prayer. This was not just a prayer for someone's blessing. Moses said, "Yet now, if thou wilt forgive their sin—; and if not, *blot me...out of thy book* which thou hast written." So great was Moses' burden, his agony, his intensity that he could not even finish the sentence. Moses offered himself. It was as if he were saying, "God, You can do anything You want with me—only save the people. If it be possible for me to bear their sin, I will." Of course his offer was rejected, for there is only one sin-bearer—that is, Christ. However, we see here a depth of prayer that few ever reach. Not many will follow the leading of the Cross to this depth, but the Apostle Paul surely did when he prayed, "I have great sorrow and unceasing pain in my heart. For I could wish that I myself were anathema from Christ for my brethren's sake" (Rom. 9:2, 3). This is not an easy path. No experience of sanctification automatically makes an intercessor, and so one must go on from death to the self-life to this deeper experience of the Cross—intercessory prayer. The cleansed vessel must be broken before the Christ within may be revealed in all His glory. The easiest but yet the hardest way of bringing the lost to Jesus is intercessory prayer. "Who follows in His train?"

In conclusion, let us sum up the three aspects of the Cross. First, we trust Christ to forgive us our sins. Secondly, we trust Christ to cleanse us from all unrighteousness and to fill us with His Holy Spirit. And thirdly, lest we begin to please ourselves, we need the daily application of the Cross, disciplining and sacrificing ourselves for the sake of Christ's kingdom to to ends of the earth.

In the following chapters we will consider in much greater detail each of these three aspects of the Cross of Christ—In chapter 2—*Christ our Substitute;* in chapters 3 and 4—*Christ our Deliverer;* in chapters 13 through 17—*The Daily Application of the Cross.* May the Spirit of God illuminate our minds as we further consider the Word of the Cross which is the power of God to those who are saved (I Cor. 1:18).

CHAPTER TWO

CHRIST CRUCIFIED *FOR* US—OUR SUBSTITUTE

> "He was wounded for *our* transgressions, he was bruised for *our* iniquities; the chastisement of *our* peace was upon him; and with his stripes *we* are healed" (Isaiah 53:5).

IN chapter 1, reference was made to the fact that the message, Christ crucified for our justification, has been quite *clearly* presented. We wonder, though, if it has been *properly* presented. Christian leaders today will readily admit that in the last generation of those who profess to be born-again Christians, something is definitely lacking. We are not now thinking of the results of modernism, liberalism, or neo-orthodoxy, but we are thinking of the product of evangelical churches. At a ministerial meeting not long ago, one of the pastors lamented the fact that though in his church there were many conversions, there was little change in the lives of the converted. Likewise, one of the best-known evangelical radio broadcasters stated that he had received letters from two leading men of evangelical circles, both of whom said they did not believe more than fifteen per cent of those who profess regeneration are really born of

God and have evidence of a vital union with Jesus Christ. This broadcaster went on to say that he would agree with the opinion of these two men. Therefore in today's presentation of the gospel something is decidedly wrong. What can it be?

Before we answer this question and consider the true meaning of salvation through the Cross of Calvary with its resultant restoration of man, we must first have a basic understanding of the Fall of Man and of its consequences. On the one hand, Eve admitted that she knew the word of God but had been deceived by the enemy and therefore had sinned; but on the other hand, Adam was not deceived (I Tim. 2:14). Adam's sin was a deliberate act of disobedience, for he knew exactly what he was doing and therefore sinned against light. He sinned with his eyes wide open, for God had said to him, "In the day that thou eatest thereof [of the tree of the knowledge of good and evil] thou shalt surely die." Adam's disobedience was a sin against the law of God, and therefore a criminal act. Adam was guilty. Immediately he died spiritually, as God had said he would. Thus Adam was "dead in trespasses and sins" and in need of forgiveness and regeneration.

The results of Adam's fall were far-reaching, for sin affected not only Adam and his own relationship with God, but also his posterity. It will be helpful, here, for us to consider the effect of the Fall in three or four different directions. *Towards God*, it brought alienation, resulting in immediate spiritual death and a delayed physical death (Gen. 2:17; 3:3; 3:19; 5:5; Rom. 5:12). While the spirit died instantly, the soul (including the mind) became greatly impaired and the body so weakened that physical death was the result. *Towards self*, it brought guilt, condemnation, and corruption. The powers of the soul were not only impaired but defiled. Thus we must bear in mind the two great facts of guilt and of depravity (Gen. 3: 8–11; Mark 7:21–23; Jer. 17:9; II Cor. 7:1). But there is also another result of the Fall that must be considered—the result *Satanward*. It brought enslavement. Our first parents had sold themselves to a subtle, cruel, crafty devil, who having brought about their fall now sought to accomplish their destruction (John 8:34; Rom. 7:14; John 10:10). Instead of having authority over all things, including the power of the enemy, they now found themselves not only weak, but enslaved. Later on, this threefoldness of the effect of the Fall would have great results *towards other members of society* as they appeared on the earth. Adam's fall would limit that love and maturity which would have enabled them to live in good and proper relationship with others.

To be complete, restoration through the atonement on Calvary must solve each of these problems of fallen man—towards God, towards self, towards Satan, and towards society. To undo the result of sin *Godward*, sinners must receive pardon and life. To undo the results of the Fall *selfward*, there must be provision for forgiveness and cleansing from all sin (actual transgressions and their defilement). There must also be provision for deliverance from the power of the world and *the devil*. There must be provision for growth in grace—proper Christian character which is necessary not only for inward victory but also for loving fellowship with *others* and for effective Christian service.

However, the provision of Calvary is full and complete. In God's great recovery program He has met every one of the needs of fallen man, including not only forgiveness and regeneration, but also deliverance from the power of the enemy, and entire sanctification resulting in Christian growth and Christian maturity. The Holy Spirit longs to bring out the proper Christian character, which is the full restoration of the image of God and that Christlikeness which every truly regenerated person longs for. We are in the process, says the Apostle Paul, of being "conformed to the image of Christ" (Rom. 8:29). Growth in Christian maturity is the process which follows the crisis of sanctification, so that right now we ought to be developing that Christian character which the Apostle John calls the wedding garment— "fine linen, bright and pure. . . the righteous acts of the saints" (Rev. 19:8).

But if, through God's great recovery program, we are to experience this wonderful and perfect restoration, we must begin at the beginning. It is absolutely essential that we have a good foundation, a proper presentation of the message of the Cross in regard to justification. And if this were the case, the result would be a better crop of Christians in this generation. Yet our lack of Christian vitality can be traced directly to faulty presentation of Christ's Gospel. Too many have been led to believe in a way of salvation which is not authorized by God's Word. While God's great recovery program is complete and meets every need of fallen man, it can be realized only on God's terms. Today, on the one hand, we have liberalism which eliminates or at least minimizes the need for conversion; on the other hand, we have "easy-believism" which offers forgiveness and regeneration without repentance and without realization of the lordship of Christ. The result is a pseudo salvation, based on either a misunderstanding of the holy love of God or on certain proof-texts of Scripture, which results in the misinterpretation and misapplication of God's great program of full salvation.

Scriptural salvation is essentially a salvation from sin. But what is sin? Sin is rebellion and enmity against God and is manifested in a threefold way: an act, an attitude, and a state. Thus stealing is an *act* of sin; hypocrisy, pride, etc., is an *attitude* of sin; being unsaved is a *state* of sin. That ample provision has been made by God for the forgiveness of sins is generally well-known. But we must not forget that this provision is available only on God's terms. He is not only Creator and Saviour, but Ruler—the God of the universe. As Ruler, He has laws, and anyone who breaks His laws is a criminal, a rebel, a betrayer of God's love, and therefore a traitor. Such a one, having committed sin, is a *sinner*. The Bible also calls him *ungodly*, "*dead* through trespasses and sins" (Eph. 2:1).

Because God is Ruler as well as Saviour, God cannot rightly and justly forgive without a proper satisfaction to public justice. This is where the message of the Cross applies: Christ *died in our stead;* He *became our Substitute;* He *took our place;* the stroke

that was *due us fell on Him* (Isa. 53:8). Because of
the death of our Substitute, God is now propitiated;
sin is now atoned for; the law is now satisfied; God
can now rightly and justly forgive every sinner who
will submit to certain self-evident terms. On God's
side the barriers to forgiveness and regeneration are
taken care of. The message of the gospel is this—that
on the ground of the love of God, Christ died instead
of the ungodly.

But on man's side what hindrances to forgiveness
and regeneration must be removed? He must admit
his guilt; be sorry for his sin; be willing to forsake
sin in every form; accept the offer of salvation on the
basis of Calvary; and receive Jesus Christ as his Lord
and Saviour. This is the way of forgiveness and of
receiving life. This is God's way of reversing guilt
and death.

Only on God's terms of repentance and trustful
surrender to Jesus Christ does God make forgiveness
and regeneration possible, for *"except ye repent*, ye
shall all likewise perish"* (Luke 13:5). Throughout
history, men of God have preached repentance as the
great need of the sinner. The forerunner of Jesus,
John the Baptist, preached repentance, saying *"Repent* ye; for the kingdom of heaven is at hand"* (Matt.
3:2). After John was delivered up, Jesus himself
came into Galilee preaching the gospel of God and
saying, *"Repent* ye, and believe in the gospel"* (Mark
1:14, 15). Then He sent out the twelve and the seventy disciples, and they went out and preached that
men should *repent* (Mark 6:12). On the day of Pentecost when the multitude, pricked in heart, asked,

"What shall we do?" Peter replied, "*Repent* ye" (Acts 2:38). Soon after, when Peter and John were used to heal the man lame from his mother's womb, Peter answered the wondering multitudes saying, "[Ye] killed the Prince of life; . . . *repent* ye therefore, and turn again" (Acts 3:15, 19). Likewise, Paul the Apostle called on the Athenians saying, "God. . . commandeth men that they should all everywhere *repent*" (Acts 17:30).

Ignorance of the need for repentance and for heart faith is well illustrated by a widow who at the graveside looked at her pastor and said, "My husband was *such a good man;* he will stand a chance, won't he?" She was seeking comfort and was basing the hope of her husband's salvation on his past goodness. But his goodness wasn't good enough and would never have atoned for past sins. Even if he could have received power to live a perfect life in the future, he still would have been faced with the guilt of his past sins. The truth of the matter is that there is no divine life without forgiveness, and there is no forgiveness without faith in the finished work of Calvary and the reception of Jesus Christ as Lord, Saviour, and Life. A good life is the result of genuine salvation but not the effectual cause; however, it is wrong to be so zealous for justification by faith that one believes a good life is unnecessary.

Let a reference to our civil courts help us understand these basic principles of salvation. Anyone who has broken a country's law is a criminal. He is apprehended, sentenced, and segregated to a place of confinement. For his release two things are necessary: First, he must serve his sentence (or a sufficient part of a sentence) so that the parole or pardoning board could conclude that for him to be released would be just as good for society as that he be retained in prison. But that is not all. Secondly, the board wants to know if he has repented. Is he sorry for his past life? Has he changed his mind? Will he be a law-abiding citizen in the future if he is paroled or pardoned? Even though a law breaker has served a sufficient portion of his sentence to warrant parole or pardon, the official board will never grant a pardon unless it is convinced that he has thoroughly repented and that he will submit to the laws of the land in the future. Even when one of our former presidents in the last days of his term of office pardoned some criminals for political reasons but not according to justice, he was greatly criticized for his actions. But certainly in God's court of the universe there is no chicanery or any way out except according to the terms that He has given. These are not arbitrary, for they have their source in the infinite wisdom of God. Thinking men know that willingness to submit to the law of the land is absolutely essential before pardoning a law-breaker. Even so, men know that God's terms are right, and that repentance and acceptance of Christ as Lord of the life are essential. God will perform a miracle when one accepts *His* terms and fully complies with them. He will not only forgive (a legal act), but will also regenerate, causing that person to be born from above, born of God. This is salvation.

Some years ago there appeared in one of the leading Christian periodicals an article under the head-

ing "Eight Ways of Dealing with Sin." After pointing out that seven methods of dealing with sin were
wrong, it named one method which it considered
right—"only believe." But in dealing with sin, "only
believe" is just as wrong as the other methods which
were rightly called false. The true gospel is *not* "only
believe." The Holy Spirit faithfully convicts of sin
and reveals our sinfulness to us in order that we may
repent, for "*if we confess* our sins, he is faithful and
righteous to forgive us our sins, and to cleanse us
from all unrighteousness." Thus, true repentance has
hope at its heart—hope as the result of seeing and of
believing that the stroke due us fell on Jesus Christ.

Here then is the first aspect of the Cross—confessing our sins and putting our faith in the Lord
Jesus Christ who died for us. Only then can God
forgive, save, regenerate, and make us new creatures
in Christ Jesus. Many will not take these steps, and
therefore many so-called Christians have only a peace
and assurance that comes through their own forgetful-
ness. They know not the peace with God which
comes by confession and cleansing through the precious blood of Christ. They are like a woman in China
who wanted to get her clothes clean. Carrying her
laundry on her head, she came to the river bank
where she was to do her washing, only to discover
that others had reached her favorite place first. Up
and down the river she walked, trying to find another
place. Every one was occupied. In the East, clothes are
soaked in water and beaten on a rock until they
take on some semblance of cleanness; then they are
bleached in the sun. This woman knew that her

laundry was in bad condition and was ashamed to open her bundle. For a while she waited, but courage did not come. Therefore, without opening her bundle she thoroughly soaked it in the river just as it was. Then she lifted it out, shook it, put it on her head, and went home again. Of course anyone would know that *her* clothes were not clean.

But sometimes we, too, do the very same thing regarding sins. We sin them one at a time, but when we come to God, we like to lump them all up together and hope that He will forgive. But the true revelation of the Holy Spirit convicts of sin and makes sin exceedingly sinful and hateful. A man under divine conviction is so anxious to be forgiven that he does not seek a short cut, but rather confesses every sin one by one as the Spirit reminds him. Then as a basis for forgiveness, he puts his faith in the shed blood of Christ and in the whole working of the atonement. Thus he not only confesses but by faith receives forgiveness. He is so in love with Christ for His wonderful goodness and so grateful to God for what He has done that from that moment on he acknowledges Jesus as Lord, and is willing to be led by His Spirit. To all such, God is pleased to perform a miracle—regeneration, being born of God, becoming a child of God.

Such a genuine experience will be witnessed to by the Holy Spirit of God. With regard to assurance of forgiveness and salvation, the child of God need not rest on a questionable doctrine but on the witness of the Holy Spirit and on vital fellowship with the Lord

Jesus Christ. Then the Holy Spirit will lead him on to deeper experiences of His grace. He will be led to see the second aspect of the Cross as the provision for sanctification.

CHAPTER THREE

CHRIST CRUCIFIED AS US—OUR DELIVERER (1)

> "[Christ] delivered us out of the
> power of darkness, and translated us
> into the kingdom of the Son of his love"
> (Col. 1:13).

A T Athens Paul's witness to the Jews in the synagogue and to others in the market place gave
him an opportunity on Mars' hill to address a whole
assembly of Jews and Greek philosophers. (This message, Acts 17:22–31, is often used in homiletics
classes as an example of a great sermon.) But the results were disappointing. Elsewhere by the power of
God, Paul had influenced great numbers to turn from
their evil ways to Christ, but in Athens there was no
great move of the Spirit. Only a few turned to Christ.

As Paul, a despised and lonely man, left Athens,
we can imagine that there were questions in his mind:
Why did not my message have its usual power? Does
the gospel not meet the need of the upper-class
Athenians? Does the gospel have a special appeal
and power for the common people only? As he made
his journey from Athens to Corinth, perhaps alone,
he carefully considered the points of his sermon. What

37

had been wrong? He had spoken on creation, repentance, resurrection, judgment, and idolatry. He had
used their own poets for illustration. What he had
said was right and good. What then was missing? He
had made *no mention of the Cross!* For that reason
Paul writes to the Corinthians:

> "And I, brethren, when I came unto you, came
> not with excellency of speech or of wisdom,
> proclaiming to you the testimony of God. For
> I determined *not to know anything among
> you, save Jesus Christ, and him crucified.* And
> I was with you in weakness, and in fear, and
> in much trembling. And my speech and my
> preaching were not in persuasive words of
> wisdom, but in demonstration of the Spirit and
> of power" (I Cor. 2:1–4).

That was it: in the preaching of the Cross there was
power; but when the Cross had been obscured or left
out altogether, there was no power. Today also, there
is definite need for the Cross to be preached in its
fullness.

As we have just seen, Christ's substitutionary
death on the Cross is for the unregenerate man and
makes possible the forgiveness of his sins and an assurance of eternal life. This is a conscious, crisis experience of new birth received when the God-given
conditions of repentance and faith are fulfilled. Soon
after this, the babe in Christ receives a revelation by
the Spirit of the need of a deeper working of Calvary.
He discovers that even though he has been converted,
sin has power over him still, and therefore he cannot do the things that he would (Gal. 5:17). He
loves the Lord and His will, yet finds himself in

bondage so that he cannot fully obey God. Within him is a contrary principle that makes it difficult for him to give instant and glad obedience to the commands of Christ. He determines to obey the Lord in all things but finds that he does not have the power to carry out his good intentions. He discovers that in many ways he is a captive. Outward victory is not so difficult to gain, but within, a battle rages. Again and again he goes down in defeat until he is almost at the point of despair.

Throughout the years in evangelical circles, only the first aspect of the Cross, *Christ crucified FOR us,* has been generally presented, while the deeper aspect of the Cross—*Christ crucified AS us* and also *IN us*—have not been so well taught. And so, not knowing God's provision for victorious living and fruitful service, many Christians have remained in bondage. Often a Christian with inner problems such as we have described is told, "This is just the normal Christian experience"; or else he is solemnly instructed, "The greater the sense of sin, the greater the advancement in the Christian life." This is not so. Praise God, there can be an end to inner conflict of the soul. God has provided a way out.

Let us then consider in detail the second aspect of the Cross—*Christ Crucified AS Us, Our Deliverer*—and thereby learn two basic facts: every Christian's *need* for the Deliverer, and the *way* of a Christian's deliverance.

A good indication of the basic trouble is found in Romans 7, especially verses 15–24, where the personal pronouns *I, me,* and *my* are repeated at least thirty-

three times. The basic problem is simply *I* trouble
or *self*-trouble.

> "That which *I* do *I* know not: for not what *I*
> would, that do *I* practise; but what *I* hate, that
> *I* do. But if what *I* would not, that *I* do, *I*
> consent unto the law that it is good. So now it
> is no more *I* that do it, but sin which dwelleth
> in *me*. For *I* know that in *me*, that is, in *my*
> flesh, dwelleth no good thing: for to will is
> present with *me*, but to do that which is good
> is not. For the good which *I* would *I* do not:
> but the evil which *I* would not, that *I* practise.
> But if what *I* would not, that *I* do, it is no more
> *I* that do it, but sin which dwelleth in *me*. *I*
> find then the law, that, to *me* who would do
> good, evil is present. For *I* delight in the law
> of God after the inward man: but *I* see a dif-
> ferent law in *my* members, warring against
> the law of *my* mind, and bringing *me* into cap-
> tivity under the law of sin which is in *my*
> members. Wretched man that *I* am! who shall
> deliver *me* out of the body of this death?"

To Paul's question, "*Who* shall deliver me?" the
answer comes, "*I thank God through Jesus Christ our
Lord.*" But the next sentence which says "So then I
of myself with the mind, indeed, serve the law of
God; but with the flesh the law of sin," reveals that
this fact of Christ as Deliverer is only mental knowledge and not heart experience. The defeated one sees
Christ as Deliverer; but then he sums up the best he
himself can do—that is, continue to live as a dual
personality (serving God with the mind, and sin with
the flesh). This is indeed a wretched state. It is the
carnal level of Christian living mentioned by Paul to
the Corinthians: "I, brethren, could not speak unto

you as unto spiritual, but as unto carnal, as unto babes in Christ" (I Cor. 3:1). They were in Christ and truly born again, but they were still carnal— walking after the manner of men, in jealousy, strife, and divisions.

These very sins are as much in evidence in the Church today as they were in Paul's time. Believers need more than the initial forgiveness of sins. They need both cleansing from sin's defilement and also deliverance from its power. Many who are living in a state of justification still have an inner agreement with sin. They have not been delivered completely from the love of sin. They may not really love sin, but they do love their own way and will sin to get it! They are still in bondage and consequently need the deliverance which Christ paid such a great price to procure for every man.

To understand better this inner conflict described so graphically in Romans 7, let us study man's original condition in the Garden of Eden, as well as man's Fall and its results, as recorded in Genesis, chapters 1, 2, and 3. God declares His eternal purpose: "Let us make man *in our image, after our likeness:* and let them have dominion. . ." (Gen. 1:26). This is what God wanted and made—a man in His image and after His likeness, someone on earth to manifest the glory of God visibly. From this eternal purpose God has never deviated, for He changes not. Today He still wants on earth a visible representative of himself: men who are "pure in heart" (Matt. 5:8), "perfect" (Matt. 5:48), and "not having spot or wrinkle or any such thing" (Eph. 5:27). On this matter, our standard, which is God's Word, is extremely plain; and its central teaching is still "Be ye *holy*." Concerning holiness, God has also said: "Follow. . . *sanctification* without which no man shall see the Lord" (Heb. 12:14); "The marriage of the Lamb is come, and his wife hath made herself ready. And it was given unto her that she should array herself in *fine linen, bright and pure:* for the fine linen is the *righteous acts* of the saints" (Rev. 19:7, 8). We need to be reminded that a holy God *must* have holy followers, and that sin must not be only forgiven but removed altogether, for "the Lamb of God . . . *taketh away* the sin of the world" (John 1: 29); He "was manifested to *take away* sins" (I John 3:5).

According to Genesis, then, God's eternal purpose was to have a man in His own image. In Genesis 2:7 we read, "Jehovah God formed man of the dust of the ground, and breathed into his nostrils the breath of life; and man became a living soul." This word *life* is in the plural—lives. God breathed into Adam both the animating principle of life and spiritual life. Thus the newly created Adam was unique, for he possessed both earthly life and also heavenly life. Through his body he had correspondence with the earth; but through his spirit, quickened by the breath of God (which is the Spirit of God), he had correspondence with heaven and so was a partaker of the divine nature. God was the center of his life. Everything revolved around God.

Of this man and his wife the Word says, "God saw everything that he had made, and behold it was very good" (Gen. 1:31). But though Adam and Eve were "very good" in their present condition, they needed to be tested. Through obedience, their innocence needed to be transformed into holiness. Even though God had breathed into them the breath of life (His Spirit), this did not mean that Adam and Eve were *filled* with the Spirit. For instance, in the New Testament Jesus Christ the Son of God breathed on the disciples and said, "Receive ye the Holy Spirit" (John 20:22); yet until Pentecost, some fifty days later, the disciples were *not filled* with the Spirit. Adam and Eve, however, had the opportunity of being filled with the Spirit through faith and obedience, even as Christians do today (though they did *not* need cleansing as we do, for they had not yet entered into conscious transgression).

Then came the awful facts of our first parents' failure and transgression (Genesis 3). As rational, self-conscious beings, they were confronted with conditions requiring the exercise of choice. To guide them aright, the Lord had carefully given them instruction and commandments. Both their endowment and environment were such as to enable them to continue in fellowship and union with God. Yet the devil, the enemy of their souls, tempted them successfully. Their first mistake was in listening to him. This resulted in the awakening of a wrong *desire,* which resulted in a wrong *choice,* which led to a wrong *act*. The Fall became an accomplished fact.

The wrong act of Adam and Eve was twofold: first, their act was disobedience to their God and Creator, and so broke fellowship and union with Him;

second, their act meant that they had yielded to, obeyed, and established a relationship, a fellowship, and a union with their unsuspected enemy, the devil, so that he whom the Scriptures call "the god of this world" (II Cor. 4:4) now became their new master.

The Fall of Man resulted then in a change of center. Up to this time God had been the center of Adam's life so that everything revolved around God. (Glance at the chart on page 50, noticing the two centers—self and Christ.) Adam's real sin was rejecting God as the center of his being, thereby elevating and substituting self as the new center and ruling principle. From then on, Adam ceased to be God-centered; now he was self-centered, a slave to Satan. Moreover, Adam's choice involved his progeny, for Adam was not only the *first* man but also the *federal head* of the human race. Because of his fall, he lost his federal headship and never regained it. Yet *his* fall involved the *fall* of the whole race, and so all his progeny manifest the same tendency of self-will and of self-centeredness. Even though Adam, we believe, was subsequently saved, he was *not* saved as the federal head of the *race* but as an individual.

And so, the evil of man's fallen nature is *selfness* or *self-centeredness*, rightly termed *depravity*, or *sinfulness of nature*. Many wrongly think of this sinfulness as the injection of a literal poison into the bloodstream, or the placement of a material substance called sin within the human nature, and that this has to be eradicated. Isaiah explains this sin principle as "all we like sheep have *gone astray*; we have turned every one to *his own way*." Therefore this sin principle may be called our *own-way-ness*—that is, the substitution of our way for God's way. Basically, fallen man is selfish. The manifestations of this are many: sometimes it is manifested in a coarse, gross way, boldly insisting on "my rights"; at other times, subtly and quietly but just as definitely, it is manifested in trying to engineer things so that self is pleased. Every single sin man can possibly commit can be traced to this basic selfness. Jesus himself bore witness to this truth, for He insisted that first of all each one of His disciples deny self. Thus He laid His axe at the very root of this *principle of sin* within man which is responsible for all his wrong doings. This selfness is the law of sin that Romans 7 speaks about.

But over and over again Paul states a great and glorious truth about deliverance. He says that when a person is saved, the old man comes to an end: "Knowing this, that *our old man was crucified* with him, that *the body of sin might be done away*, that so we should no longer be in bondage to sin" (Rom. 6:6). Strictly speaking, the *old man* died when Christ died. This great fact becomes our heritage when we are saved. Paul, however, seemed to anticipate both our blindness and our unwillingness to accept and believe this truth; and so he adds proof after proof in this wonderful sixth chapter of Romans to establish the fact in our minds that for the Christian the old man *was crucified* (vs. 6), *has died* (vs. 7), and *has been buried* (vs. 4). Our part is to reckon on this great fact. We are not to make it true, for it is *not* a matter of imagination but of reckoning on the unalterable Word of God. When we are born again we *are* new creatures in Christ Jesus, for "if any man is in Christ, he is a new creature: the old things are passed away; behold, they are become new" (II Cor. 5:17).

It is a sad fact that simply because the majority of Christians do not know the truth of their deliverance, they still are *dominated by their former manner of life*. But God says, "*Put away*, as concerning your former manner of life, *the old man*, ... and *put on the new man*, that after God hath been created in righteousness and holiness of truth" (Eph. 4:22, 24). This is another way of saying, "Reckon ye also yourselves to be dead unto sin, but alive unto God" (Rom. 6:11.)

In the former manner of life before our renewal through the redemption of Christ, the old man directed the life, allowing the flesh to have its way, so that the whole being was largely, if not entirely, ruled by its appetites, desires, passions, and senses. Many are confused just here, thinking the flesh and the old man are the same, but they are not the same. The old man comes to an end when a person is saved, so that for the Christian, the old man is crucified, dead, and buried. On this fact we are told to reckon, count, believe.

On the other hand, nowhere in Scripture does it say that the flesh (human nature) is dead, though it does speak of the flesh being crucified: "they ... have crucified the flesh with the passions and the lusts thereof" (Gal. 5:24). There is nothing essentially wrong with the flesh except when living for itself. The only time flesh or human nature is wrong and sinful is when it rules. God never intended the flesh to rule but rather the Spirit; and when the Spirit rules, the flesh is pure and right. But the flesh *allowed to rule* is anarchy.

Romans 8 speaks of "the mind of the flesh," but reference to the original makes it clear that Paul says it is *the minding of the flesh* that is enmity against God. "The mind [the minding] of the flesh is death; . . . because the mind [minding] of the flesh is enmity against God; for it is not subject to the law of God, neither indeed can it be: and they that are in the flesh cannot please God" (Rom. 8:6–8). This word is plain enough so that it needs no explanation. Luther used to say, "Do not tell me what the Word means; tell me what the Word says." As clearly as possible, this passage states that the end result of continuing in this wretched state of minding the flesh is *death!*

Galatians 5:24 gives the solution to our awful problem: "They that are of Christ Jesus have crucified the flesh with the passions and lusts thereof." The Cross is the answer. The Cross is not only the place where Christ died, and not only the place my old man died and came to an end, but the Cross is also the place for the flesh. The flesh as a ruling principle must be crucified and be deposed, and the Spirit of Christ enthroned as the very center of the life. This is the only solution. We do not get far by saying less of the flesh or less of self. The flesh must be deposed altogether. *God never intended the flesh to rule.* It was only after the Fall that the flesh began to rule the life; so we need to be saved not from sin and hell only, but also from our own deranged nature, and from the dominance of the flesh. The flesh is crucified in the sense that its dominion is ended and its place of rulership given to the Spirit, who wants our spirit dominating and our body a willing servant. While the flesh is ruling, it accumulates many new garments or habits which must be put off.

Yes, the Fall of Man in Eden brought disaster to the human race. But the most hopeful thing about this disaster of Eden is that it was *God's child* who was in the wreck. Let this simple illustration illuminate this point. The engineer of Train No. 1 had a running order from his father, who was the train dispatcher, to take a certain siding and wait for Train No. 2. He disobeyed his order and a collision resulted. The news of the disaster flashed over the wires, including the fact that the engineer of Train No. 1 was pinned under his engine and would die if not soon rescued. Calling the division superintendent, the father demanded a "special" and also a wrecking crew at once, exclaiming, "*My son* is in the wreck! *My son* is in the wreck! I know he disobeyed my order, but he's *my child*, and he's under the engine. Man, can't you understand? Give me that train quick! A thousand dollars, did you say? No matter what it costs, order that train! My life for his life!"

What truth is revealed when this story is applied spiritually! In the Garden of Eden, God's son (Adam) disobeyed orders and was in a wreck. But because he was God's child, he *must* be delivered—no matter the cost to the Father. Thus, foreseeing the disaster of man's disobedience before the foundation of the world, God, with His father-heart, took command of the forces of heaven and earth, and then, to rescue His child, himself suffered death and conquered hell—offering His life for a life! And so, in the person of Jesus Christ, God came to earth as the last Adam, as the representative of the human race, identified himself with man and also with sin, and then bore the sinner and his sin to an awful death on the Cross and then into the grave. There He brought this old creation to an end. "Him who knew no sin he *made to be sin* on our behalf" (II Cor. 5:21).

Jesus came, then, to be not only our Saviour but our Deliverer. At Nazareth He entered the synagogue and read from the book of the prophet Isaiah concerning himself: "The Spirit of the Lord is upon me, because he anointed me to preach good tidings to the poor: he hath sent me *to proclaim release* to the captives, and recovering of sight to the blind, *to set at liberty* them that are bruised, to proclaim the acceptable year of the Lord" (Luke 4:18, 19). Afterwards He said, "Today hath this scripture been fulfilled in your ears" (Luke 4:21). Christ came into the world not only to forgive sins and give eternal life, but also to bring release to those who are in bondage to self-will and to set at liberty those that are bruised by the devil.

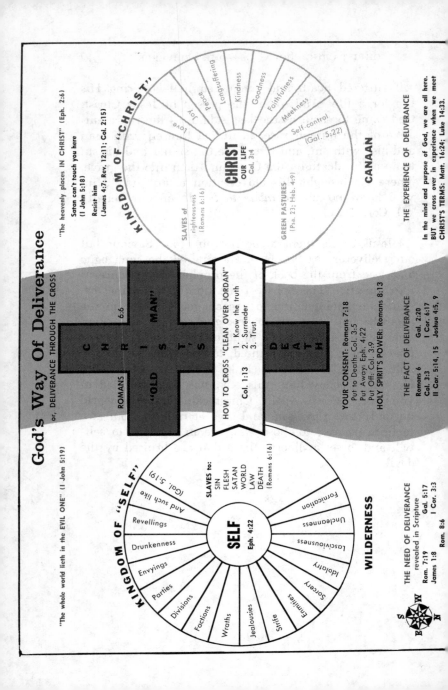

God's Way Of Deliverance
or, DELIVERANCE THROUGH THE CROSS

"The whole world lieth in the EVIL ONE" (1 John 5:19)

"The heavenly places IN CHRIST" (Eph. 2:6)

Satan can't touch you here
(1 John 5:18)

Resist him
(James 4:7; Rev. 12:11; Col. 2:15)

KINGDOM OF "CHRIST"

CHRIST
OUR LIFE
Col. 3:4

Love
Joy
Peace
Longsuffering
Kindness
Goodness
Faithfulness
Meekness
Self-control
(Gal. 5:22)

SLAVES of
righteousness
(Romans 6:16)

GREEN PASTURES
(Psa. 23; Heb. 4:9)

CANAAN

THE EXPERIENCE OF DELIVERANCE

In the mind and purpose of God, we are all here.
BUT we cross over in experience when we meet
CHRIST'S TERMS: Matt. 16:24; Luke 14:33.

ROMANS   6:6

CHRIST'S
"OLD"   "MAN"
DEATH

HOW TO CROSS "CLEAN OVER JORDAN"
1. Know the truth
2. Surrender
3. Trust
Col. 1:13

YOUR CONSENT: Romans 7:18
Put to Death: Col. 3:5
Put Away: Eph. 4:22
Put Off: Col. 3:9
HOLY SPIRIT'S POWER: Romans 8:13

THE FACT OF DELIVERANCE

Romans 6   Gal. 2:20
Col. 3:3   I Cor. 6:17
II Cor. 5:14, 15   Joshua 4:5, 9

KINGDOM OF "SELF"

SLAVES to:
SIN
FLESH
SATAN
WORLD
LAW
DEATH
(Romans 6:16)

SELF
Eph. 4:22

And such like
(Gal. 5:19)
Revellings
Drunkenness
Envyings
Parties
Divisions
Factions
Wraths
Jealousies
Strife
Enmities
Sorcery
Idolatry
Lasciviousness
Uncleanness
Fornication

WILDERNESS

THE NEED OF DELIVERANCE
revealed in Scripture
Rom. 7:19   Gal. 5:17
James 1:8   I Cor. 3:3
               Rom. 8:6

S
W   E
N

CHAPTER FOUR

CHRIST CRUCIFIED *AS* US—OUR DELIVERER (2)

> "The *truth* shall make you free"
> (John 8:32).
> "The *Son* shall make you free"
> (John 8:36).

EVERY Christian has experienced forgiveness of sins and has assurance of eternal life. But every Christian has *not* experienced deliverance from the self-life. "Self," William Law said, "is the whole evil of man's fallen nature." Self is expressed in the desire to have and maintain one's own way and one's own rights—instead of giving them up as Jesus enjoined. Yet because one who is full of self can *not* be filled with the Spirit, any salvation that will truly meet the need of fallen man *must* deliver from the power of the self-life. Indeed it is in this connection and to meet this very need that the Holy Spirit reveals to the hungry a deeper meaning in the Cross of Christ— *Christ Crucified AS Us*.

Although almost every Christian admits some need of deliverance from bondage to the self-life and to the devil, in most cases the realization of this need

has not become acute. For instance, one who had
been faithfully witnessed to freely admitted her self-
centered condition but excused herself by saying,
"I am jealous and irritable and self-centered, I know;
but I had the experience of salvation when I was a
little girl. When most other Christians are manifestly
living for themselves, why should I be bothered about
my self-centeredness?" The Church of God today certainly needs the "recovering of sight to the blind,"
for the Bible pointedly says, "Whosoever *doeth* not
righteousness is *not* of God" (I John 3:10). Small
wonder, then, that these words of God in John's
Epistle so shocked an honest and awakened soul,
that one day she cried out, "Either this Word of
God is not true, or else we are not Christians."

Again and again in both the Old and New Testaments God declares His standard for men. In his
first letter the Apostle Peter says, "Like as he who
called you is holy, be ye yourselves also holy *in all
manner of living*" (I Peter 1:15). This refers not to
positional holiness but to practical, everyday holy
living. This is impossible to the natural man, for all
descendants of our fallen parents, Adam and Eve, find
themselves hopelessly in bondage to the self-life.
(Peter calls it the "vain manner of life handed down
from [our] fathers," and Paul calls it the "old man.")
But for man's lack there is a God-given provision
which Peter declares in I Peter 1:18, 19: "Ye were
redeemed...with precious blood, as of a lamb without blemish and without spot, even the blood of
Christ." Here, then, is God's great answer for our
desperate need of deliverance—*Christ has redeemed us*
from that selfishness handed down from our fathers.

We have stated that the first step in deliverance is the realization that God has been aware of our problem and has already made provision according to our need. To work out deliverance by our own resolution or determination is impossible. By grace *through faith* we are delivered from the self-life, even as we are saved by grace through faith. As federal head of the whole race (a headship lost by the first Adam and then transferred to the last Adam), Christ bore us to Calvary and died as our representative. We were identified with Him in His death. Paul's testimony is our testimony—"I *have been* crucified [together] with Christ." Here then is God's method of dealing with the sinfulness of our nature— "our old man *was* crucified with him" (Rom. 6:6). Thus at Calvary, not only Christ was crucified and died, but *we* were crucified and *we* died; there, not only Christ was buried, but *we* were buried. Ever since Calvary, God has been through with our old man. As far as God is concerned, when a person is saved, the old man comes to an end. This wonderful truth Paul states over and over again in Romans 6.

To the soul who really hungers and thirsts for righteousness and is seeking a way out from his conflict in soul, God reveals that Jesus died as his representative: "One died for all, therefore *all* died" (II Cor. 5:14); "ye died" (Col. 3:3). This is God's truth for *every single person*, just as Christ's substitutionary death is for every person. Positionally, *all* are dead. Jesus Christ crucified is the ground of deliverance, the very same as He is the ground of salvation, so that all salvation and all deliverance is dependent upon what Jesus already accomplished on the Cross two thousand years ago. Yet just as only those who definitely accept Him as Saviour are saved, so only those who reckon Christ's death as their death actually experience the crucifixion of the old man. Romans 6:10, 11 says, "The death that he died, he died unto sin *once*: ... *Even so reckon ye also* yourselves to be dead unto sin."

Some think that reckoning oneself to be dead to sin is a daily dying unto sin, but the context shows that it is not so. Reckoning self dead to sin is a definite crisis experience. The Word says that Christ "died unto sin *once*." Even so, we are to reckon ourselves to be dead to sin (Rom. 6:10, 11). Having died with Christ is a fact whether it has yet become true in one's experience or not. If our daily experience requires a new decision every day, it is because we have not settled the issue, utterly denied self, and renounced all that we have. In spite of the Word's telling us to "make not provision for the flesh, to fulfil the lusts thereof" (Rom. 13:14), we are still making provision for the flesh somewhere.

In Galatians 5:19–21 Paul catalogues the works (sins) which are the result of a flesh-controlled life. Let us go through the whole list one by one: "The works of the flesh are manifest, which are these: fornication, uncleanness, lasciviousness" (these are the terrible sins of impurity). Next in the list is "idolatry." Any idol (any thing we put in place of God) is an indication that we are still controlled by the flesh; and the flesh we have already learned, is incapable of guiding the life aright. All self-seeking (which is self-love) is really self-worship, and *self-*

worship is idolatry of the grossest form. For instance, too often we cannot give an immediate answer to the leading of God because we must first bow to ask permission from our idol (family, money, security, comfort). Truly this form of idolatry is subtle, but so often it is the chief hindrance to obeying God. On the contrary, when the Apostle Paul was called, he "conferred not with flesh and blood" but obeyed instantly.

Next in Paul's list of sins resulting from a flesh-controlled life come the following: "sorcery, enmities, strife, jealousies, wraths" (Gal. 5:20). Thus, if we are angry with our brother, if we have any grudges, if we are irritable and self-centered, the flesh is in control. In this state we need more than forgiveness. We need deliverance from the dominance of the flesh-life. It must be deposed, and the Spirit given His rightful place. The flesh *in control* leads to "wraths," as well as to the remainder of the sins in the list: "factions, divisions, parties, envyings, drunkenness, revellings, and such like" (Gal. 5:20, 21). In conclusion, we might list other expressions of the self-life in control, like touchiness, impatience, anxiety, laziness, gossip, resentment, levity, self-pity, self-love, self-esteem, criticism, pride, dishonesty. All these terrible sins stem from the center of self. (Perhaps a glance at the chart at the beginning of this chapter will clarify this point.) Certainly when self is the center, we cannot expect anything worthwhile to develop in the life.

To help discover ourselves to ourselves, to open our eyes to our true condition, we might ask our-

selves these five questions: Am I absolutely truthful?
Am I absolutely honest? Am I absolutely pure? Am
I easily offended? Am I living for something really
worthwhile? If we find evidence of the works of the
flesh in us and cannot give the right answer to these
questions, it is a positive indication that we have not
been delivered. We are still walking after the flesh.

Until the issue is settled and there is a definite
break with bondage to the flesh, this experience of
inner conflict is a wretched state, for in this condition
the Bible says "ye may not do the things that ye
would" (Gal. 5:17). A person who is born again may
not altogether go into sin, for the Spirit is there; but
on the other hand, unless the flesh has been deposed,
the Holy Spirit can not have His way completely,
for the flesh insists on ruling. Because one in this
state cannot be altogether bad or altogether good, this
condition often ends in confusion, frustration, and
sometimes even insanity.

Paul gives us an awful warning that to continue
in this state of duality is not only truly wretched and
wicked, but dangerous. He says, "Of which I forewarn you, even as I did forewarn you, that *they who
practise such things shall not inherit the kingdom of
God*" (Gal. 5:21). This is God's Word.

"But I am saved!" you say. "I know I am a
Christian."

That makes no difference. The Bible says very
plainly that if these things continue in your life, you
shall *not* inherit the kingdom of God.

"But wasn't I truly saved?"

Yes, you may have been, but this is a dangerous state you are in now, and you must settle this matter of whether you are going to walk after the flesh or after the Spirit.

You reply, "Oh, it can't mean that."

All right. Try to get peace of heart by changing the Word of God. You will never get it that way. The only way you will get real peace of heart is to agree with the Word of God and appropriate the blessings and benefits of Calvary. The reason God tells us plainly that these awful things are the result of the flesh-controlled life is to bring us to admit our sin, confess it, and receive the deliverance He offers us. May the Holy Spirit of God so convict us that we will be willing to accept the truth. Real repentance is simply being honest before God, opening up our hearts and calling the things we find there by their right names. We must turn from sin and be willing to hate what He hates and love what He loves. God hates the works of the flesh; God hates sin. And we, too, must be willing to hate the works of the flesh (self-life) and to hate sin so that we will be ready to meet the conditions for the wonderful deliverance that He has provided through Christ's so great salvation.

Better than any other passage of Scripture, perhaps, Galatians 5:16–25 explains not only the two contrary principles at work (in those who have not yet found victory), but also God's solution for the inner conflict.

"I say, Walk by the Spirit, and ye shall not fulfil the lust of the flesh, for the flesh lusteth against the Spirit, and the Spirit against the flesh; for *these are contrary the one to the other; that ye may not do the things that ye would"* (Gal. 5:16, 17).

To be delivered from bondage to self and to the devil, we see the absolute necessity of a *definite* choice. We, too, as Adam, are confronted with conditions requiring the exercise of choice. The issue in our case, as it was with Adam, is that of *choosing* Christ or self. It is on the basis of the redemption of Jesus Christ that we *can* and *must choose* to walk after the Spirit instead of after the flesh. We cannot obey the Spirit *and* the flesh, for these are contrary to each other. We must choose one of two roads: the road of the self-life or the road of the Christ-life.

Self-will Road is broad and smooth at the beginning, but the pleasures of the world and the satisfaction enjoyed through self-pleasing prove to be all too temporary. Soon both the pseudo-freedom and counterfeit happiness are dimmed by fruits of unrighteousness, such as inner conflict, jealousy, resentment, touchiness, dissatisfaction, self-pity, rebellion, irritability, unbelief, hypocrisy, selfishness, criticism, despair, impurity, and a host of other sins that eventually destroy peace of heart.

The other road, the Christ-way Road, may begin narrow, at least from the world's point of view, but it is not too narrow for one who has yielded all to Christ. On this road we find the fruits of righteousness such as victory, peace, joy, satisfaction, rest, assurance, purity, brokenness, sacrificing love, power, fruitfulness, and other blessings both temporal and eternal. The crowning joy will be at the end of the road when faith turns to a face-to-face sight of Jesus himself.

This choice of roads is a crisis experience, a sort of second crossroad. At the time when we make our initial choice—the choice of our eternal destiny—we receive Christ as Saviour from past sins and Lord of our life for the future. Generally, however, the full implications of salvation are not understood until later. As we have seen, the second choice or issue is between *Christ* and *self* as absolute ruler in our present life. But these are mutually exclusive, for to choose Christ is to make a complete renunciation of self, which has ruled for years and built up unnatural appetites, passions, and desires that still clamor for attention. Christ can never be our deliverer from the "vain manner of life handed down from our fathers" unless we make a complete renunciation of all we *are* and of all we *have*. The flesh must be deposed; in other words, we must renounce all allegiance to the first Adam and all he fell into. This old way of life must be entirely set aside so that the Spirit of Christ may be enthroned as the new ruling principle and may lead us into the new life, a life of union with the last Adam, the Son of God, our Lord Jesus Christ.

Many claim to be disciples of Jesus Christ who have not denied themselves and taken up the cross to follow Him. They have changed the level of their living, but they are still living for self. God has given us a wonderful illustration of our deliverance from the self-life in Israel's crossing of the Jordan River on their way to Canaan. We read that

> "when the people removed from their tents, to
> pass over the Jordan, . . . and the feet of the
> priests that bare the ark were dipped in the
> brink of the water, . . . the waters which came
> down from above stood, and rose up in one
> heap, a great way off, . . . and those that went
> down toward the. . . Salt Sea, were wholly cut
> off: . . . and all Israel passed over on dry
> ground, until all the nation were passed clean
> over the Jordan" (Josh. 3:14–17).

In considering what this account has to teach us,
it is interesting to notice first that the water rose up
in a heap thirty miles upstream at the city of *Adam*.
Nothing is unimportant in Scripture, not even names.
The fact that the cutting off of the flow of the river
was *at the city of Adam* is God's way of telling us
that the power of the Cross avails right back to our
forefather Adam. From this vain life handed down
from our father, we have been redeemed with the
precious blood of Christ (I Pet. 1:18, 19). Thus Christ's
redemption touches *original* as well as *actual* sin.
Praise God.

Consider secondly that Israel's deliverance was
gained by a definite act of crossing Jordan. One specific
morning the Israelites left their tents on purpose to
cross the river. Perhaps many times before, the Israelites had left their tents for other reasons. But there
came a time when they left them on purpose to cross
over Jordan. In obedience to God's command, they also
took twelve stones from the old side of the river and
deposited them in the river bed.

> "Joshua set up twelve stones *in the midst of
> the Jordan*, in the place where the feet of the

priests... stood: and they are there unto this day" (Josh. 4:9).

Even so, by one definite act we must commit our old man to the Cross. We too are literally to hand ourselves over to Christ in a full surrender so that He may crucify the old man. (We have said before that the crucifixion of the old man was a fact. This positional truth must now become actual and personal.) Because He has given us a free will, He waits for this surrender and full consecration. If we want to, we can refuse and resist and defy God to His face. Yet in His love and mercy He will patiently wait for us, and will bring about experiences, circumstances, and conditions to cause us to *will* to surrender ourselves wholly into His hands. He wants to make the Cross real in our experience. He wants the Cross to stand between us and the old life as definitely as the Jordan River ran between Israel and the wilderness life.

But Israel also took twelve stones from the river's bed to the Canaan side for a memorial.

> "Joshua said unto them, ... take you up every man of you a stone upon his shoulder, according unto the number of the tribes of the children of Israel" and they "took up twelve stones *out of the midst* of the Jordan, ... and they carried them over with them unto the place where they lodged, and laid them down there. And those twelve stones, which they took out of the Jordan, did Joshua set up in Gilgal" (Josh. 4:5, 8, 20).

Our experience of sanctification must be just as vital, definite, and conclusive as it was for Israel,

of whom the Word says that they "were passed
clean over the Jordan." The Israelites crossed over
into a new land. On the other side of Jordan everything was new. They no longer lived by the manna
or by water out of the rock. No longer were they
wandering about in the wilderness—wandering and
oftentimes wondering. They were to live on the old
corn of the land, to enter into their very own land
which God himself had deeded to them when He
promised Joshua, "There shall not any man be able
to stand before thee all the days of thy life: as I
was with Moses, so I will be with thee; I will not
fail thee, nor forsake thee. Be strong and of good
courage" (Josh. 1:5, 6). Here Joshua was given an
assurance of God's presence so that He would make
Israel's way prosperous and they would have good success. In other words, they were given an assurance
of victory in every situation.

As Christians, having crossed our Jordan (the
Cross), we have Christ as our new center, who
so rules us through the Holy Spirit that we will manifest the fruit of the Spirit—"love, joy, peace, longsuffering, kindness, goodness, faithfulness, meekness,
self-control" (Gal. 5:22). The Spirit-walk is a walk
according to the will of God, while the flesh-walk is
simply a walk according to our own desires. What a
contrast between the fruit of the Spirit and the works
of the flesh! What a difference! Yes, the fruit of the
Spirit is what we want and that is a natural result,
not of striving after these good things, but of a right
relationship to Jesus Christ and His Holy Spirit—of
walking by the Spirit. Romans 8 gives the only satis-
factory answer to the problem of our deranged nature:

the "I" of Romans 7 has been changed for the Spirit of Christ, who is offered to take the place of the law of sin and death which we inherit from our father Adam. Romans 8:2–4 says,

> "The law of the Spirit of life in Christ Jesus made me free from the law of sin and of death. For what the law could not do, in that it was weak through the flesh, God, sending his own Son in the likeness of sinful flesh and for sin, condemned sin in the flesh: that the ordinance of the law might be fulfilled in us, who walk not after the flesh, but after the Spirit."

The possibility of walking by the Spirit is plainly set forth in God's Word, and this is what every Christian should seek—not only for occasional times of need, but as a settled, consistent way of life.

Is this experience a state of grace from which we *cannot* fall? No! But it is a state of grace from which we *need not* fall. It is simply Jesus delivering us from inward agreement with self-pleasing, and trusting Jesus to keep us from sin. It is renunciation of the love of sin. We all know He can keep us from *some* sin. But if we have fully yielded to Him, it is no harder for Him to keep us from *all* sin. Anything less than this is making provision for the flesh to fulfill the lusts thereof. Even though the old life is ended and the new life begun, the Christian must still keep choosing to walk not after the flesh, as in the past, but by the Spirit. Instead of changing His Word to conform with our lives, we must trust the Spirit of God to change our lives to conform with His Word.

In conclusion, let us state briefly the three steps that have been helpful to souls seeking the victorious life: first, *know;* second, *surrender;* third, *trust.* First, *know* that there is a way of deliverance. God's redemption in the Person of Jesus Christ is full and complete. It is for all to get rightly related and adjusted to what Jesus has already done. Many come and take only the forgiveness of sins. Some come and take a little deeper measure of victory, but God wants us to have the full value of the death of Christ. God's table is spread. All things are ready. His invitation is to come and "according to your faith be it done unto you" (Matt. 9:29).

Second, *surrender.* Consecrate your life to Christ in total abandonment so that He can make the Cross real in your experience. Believe not only in an outward Cross but an inward Cross. Actually go through the Cross as Jesus did. Let the Cross set you free from all bondage. "If therefore the Son shall make you free, ye shall be free indeed." Deny yourself—nail the disposition to have your own way to the Cross. Then you will find that you are not only dead to sins (if you are a Christian at all, your attitude must be that of being dead to sins), but you will be delivered literally "out of the power of darkness, and translated. . . into the kingdom of the Son of his love" (Col. 1:13). This truth, which is positional for all, will now become experiential. You will have a right to say no to the devil. You will have a right to say no to the claims of the old life.

Third, *trust* God to accept and deliver as you yield fully to Him. Trust the Holy Spirit to apply and make real *in* you all that God in Christ has done *for* you. This then is God's redemption. This is His way of deliverance. The Son of God died for you and His blood bought you. His redemption is far greater than the results of the Fall, for if "by the trespass of the one, death reigned through the one; *much more* shall they that receive the abundance of grace and of the gift of righteousness reign in life through the one, even Jesus Christ" (Rom. 5:17). "Wherefore also he is able to save to the uttermost them that draw near unto God through him, seeing he ever liveth to make intercession for them" (Heb. 7:25).

God's Eternal Purpose For Man

"GOD SAID, LET US MAKE MAN IN OUR IMAGE, AFTER OUR LIKENESS..." (GEN. 1:26)

"...YE SHALL BE HOLY, FOR I AM HOLY". (I PET. 1:16).

CHRIST CRUCIFIED

Christ in heaven

Adam before the fall

Incarnation Phil. 2:6

Christ on earth

Eph. 1: 9-11, 3:11, 4:12-13

SINLESS
Gen. 2:25
untested

SINLESS
Heb. 4:15
tested

Adam's fall

"MADE SIN" II Cor. 5:21

SIN AND FLESH LEVEL

natural man by birth

Rom. 5:12-17

"Him who knew no sin he made to be sin on our behalf; that we might become the righteousness of God in him" (II Cor. 5:21).

SINFUL HUMAN RACE

"RAISED WITH HIM" Eph. 2:6

"new creation"—"all things new." II Cor. 5:17

SPIRITUAL LEVEL by faith—Rom. 8:14, Col. 1:10 increasing

"He that saith he abideth in him ought himself also to walk even as he walked" (I John 2:6).

FREE FROM SIN—Rom. 6:1,2, 3
James 1:2, 3
Rom. 6:18, 22   Rom. 8:11
I Cor. 10:13
being tested

II Cor. 5:1, 4

CARNAL LEVEL
by choice or ignorance

Rom. 6:13 "present members"
Rom. 12:1 "present bodies"

Rom. 6:4, 5, 6   I Pet. 4:1

CHAPTER FIVE

GOD'S ETERNAL PURPOSE FOR MAN

> "Making known . . . the mystery of his
> will, . . . according to the eternal pur-
> pose which he purposed in Christ Jesus
> our Lord:. . . till we all attain . . . unto
> a fullgrown man, unto the measure of
> the stature of the fulness of Christ"
> (Eph. 1:9; 3:11; 4:13).

TO learn further of God's wondrous plan for man's salvation to the uttermost, let us approach the second aspect of the Cross—Christ Crucified AS Us— from the viewpoint of God's eternal will for man.

In the first chapter of the first book of the Bible, God makes known His eternal purpose for man in the words, "Let us make man in *our* image, after *our* likeness" (Gen. 1:26). This was what God wanted, and this was what God made—a man in His own image, after His own likeness. God wanted a man on earth to manifest the glory of God visibly. From this eternal purpose for creating man, He has never deviated, for Jehovah "changeth not." Though man's Fall made redemption necessary, it did not annul or change His purpose. Redemption was not God's afterthought, for long before man fell, even before his creation, provision for his restoration had been made. Therefore the central teaching of God's Word is still *"Be ye holy, for I am holy"* (I Pet. 1:16 A.V.); and *"Walk even as he walked"* (I John 2:6). This is what God expects, and this is what God provided—salvation to the uttermost, made possible through the redemption of Christ. Any other salvation is an illusion.

The reason man in his first estate was pronounced "very good" was a lack of evil rather than a definite choosing of good. But God wanted man to exercise his power of will and definitely choose to be God-like and holy. Yet to be like God man must be like Him in will, and so Adam was given his own free will to make a deliberate choice (perhaps a series of choices) by which he would transform his state of innocency into holiness.

From Genesis 3, we know that in the hour of testing, Adam did not stand. He fell. The effects of this fall were far-reaching. Adam and Eve became dead to God but alive to sin and the flesh. Truly their eyes were opened. Thus through Adam "sin entered into the world, and *death through sin;* and so *death passed unto all men,* for that all sinned" (Rom. 5:12). Adam was more than just the first man on earth; he was the head of the whole human race so that in Adam the whole race fell from a sinless level, where there was fellowship and communion with God, to a new level of sin and to a break in relationship with God. This new level to which Adam and the race fell is the sin and flesh level—the carnal level—where man lives for self. On this level all men are born into the world. On this level sin is inevitable.

In the chart at the beginning of this chapter we have sought to illustrate these truths. Glance at the *blue* line from left to right. This line is the level upon which God intended His man to walk. We have drawn it with an upward trend, for God's intention was that man should constantly *advance*—"increasing in the knowledge of God" (Col. 1:10). This increase was to have begun in the life of Adam and, we believe, will continue through all eternity—as God unfolds His treasures, the mysteries of His love and of His grace. It represents God's purpose of fellowship and communion for the man whom He had created.

It is evident that God knew that the Fall would occur. He had made provision for it long before the Creation by the Lamb "slain from the foundation of the world" (Rev. 13:8 A.V.). But for this provision to become actual history, the eternal Word of God had to leave heaven, come to earth, become flesh, and be the first to walk on the sinless level—the same level on which Adam walked before the Fall: "Christ Jesus . . . , existing in the form of God, counted not the being on an equality with God a thing to be grasped [clung to], but emptied himself, taking the form of a servant, *being made in the likeness of men*" (Phil. 2:5–7). (See the yellow line at the upper left-hand side of the chart—it continues on in the *blue* line.) Jesus met on earth every temptation and every trial that Adam *should* have met (and that he *would* have met had he not fallen). And in all points He was tempted like as we are, and yet, God says, "without sin" (Hebrews 4:15). Jesus did *not* fall. Surely such a

One who himself hath suffered being tempted is able
to succor us who are tempted (Heb. 2:18).

Having fully finished the earthly testings, on the
day of His death Jesus stepped down from the sinless
level to the sin and flesh level, for He was made to
be sin on our behalf (II Cor. 5:21). (Notice that the
blue line on the chart descends just before the Cross
to a *black* line.) Just as soon as Jesus touched *our*
sin, just as soon as He took sin upon himself, He died—
"obedient unto death, yea, even the death of the cross"
(Phil. 2:8). That was Calvary!

Most of us have not had any difficulty in believing
or understanding that we were all involved in Adam's
fall, and that we were born not in the image of
God but in the fallen image of Adam. This is depravity and is clearly manifested by our *weakened*
bodies, our *impaired* minds, and our *disturbed* emotions. It is also manifested in that a child becomes committed to selfishness even before reason has developed.
Thus the Bible categorically states that *everyone
chooses* sin: *"All* we like sheep *have gone astray"*
(Isa. 53:6). This is because of the depravity mentioned above and also because of the devil's temptations, the pull of the world, and almost universal
example of selfishness. We must bear in mind that we
are born into an anti-Christ, pro-self world, and the result of choosing self (selfness, selfishness) is moral depravity—depravity of the free will. Each man becomes
a voluntary transgressor and verily guilty.

Though Adam was the federal head of the human
race, the representative man, he was but the "figure

of him that was to come" (Rom. 5:14), for the real
head is the last Adam, Christ. Yet if Adam, the figure,
could take the whole human race into sin, surely
Christ, the substance of that figure, could take the
whole race back to God. As Jesus Christ hung on
the Cross of Calvary, He died not only *for* us (our
Substitute), but *as* us (our Representative). He was
united with the human race and became our representative so that when He hung on that Cross, we
hung there with Him. When He died, we died. When
He was buried, we were buried. As far as God is
concerned, at Calvary the sinful human race was
crucified, dead, and buried. "We were buried therefore with him through baptism into death" (Rom.
6:4).

The varying attitudes of men and of God toward
Christ's death is illuminating. Had *Pilate* cared to
write an inscription on the stone at the door of the
sepulcher, he would have written, "Here lies Jesus,
King of the Jews." If the *Scribes and Pharisees* had
written the epitaph, they would have written, "Here
lies the impostor who claimed to be the Son of God."
Had *Satan* written the inscription, it would have read,
"Jesus of Nazareth, whom I have overcome." But if
God had written the inscription, it would have read,
"Here lies the sinful human race." This then is the
deeper meaning of Christ's death. Jesus himself was
crucified; but the Bible account declares that "with
him were two others, malefactors, one on either side."
The truth is that far more than two others were crucified with Him, for He identified himself with the
whole sinful race. He bore us *all* to Calvary. In the
person of Christ we *all* died.

There should be no difficulty in understanding this truth, for we all accept this fact of federal headship in the matter of the Fall. Adam acted for the whole human race so that when he chose sin rather than obedience, he, the head of the race, plunged all of us to that sin and flesh level (See the lower *black* line with its downward trend.) Genesis 5:1 and 3 clearly tell us that though Adam was created in the likeness of God, Adam's posterity was begotten in his own likeness. After the Fall this likeness was therefore a fallen likeness, so that we are all born "fallen," which is really not our fault but our calamity. We are not considered guilty simply because we are born in the image of fallen Adam. We are guilty because by sin of our own we endorse Adam's sin and fall. No one is condemned for being born in Adam's fallen image, but on the contrary for rejecting Christ as man's Saviour from this heredity. Our condemnation is for persisting in going our own way, for endorsing Adam's sin by sinning. We have become sinners by practice and therefore are guilty before God.

It is exactly this same principle with regard to endorsing Christ's death on Calvary. Positionally, we were all taken there; in the mind of God the whole human race died with Christ. But as we endorsed Adam's sin by sinning and thus became guilty sinners, so now we must endorse *Christ's death* by dying to sin and self. Only in this way do we renounce all that Adam entered into by his sin and fall. Jesus struck at the very heart of this fact when He said, "If any man would come after me, let him *deny himself*" (Matt. 16:24). "Whosoever he be of you who renounceth not all that he hath, he cannot be my disciple" (Luke 14:33).

It is possible to know all these great truths and still be entirely without the benefits they confer. To believe in our identification with Christ in His death in an abstract way is not enough. It must be experiential. Let us keep in mind that we become guilty when we endorse Adam's sin by sinning, but we are forgiven and delivered when we endorse Christ's death and resurrection by dying and being raised with Him. Jesus says that denial of self (giving up of all personal rights, renouncing everything that belongs to the old life—in other words, a complete about-face) is a step *we* must take. Only then will the Holy Spirit make this great truth real in our personal experience so that we will receive its full benefit—namely, ability to live unto God, and deliverance from the power of sin, of the devil, and of the world.

But if Adam, the figure of Him who was to come, could work such havoc with the race, taking us all down to sin (the level colored black), Christ, the Substance of that figure, can do infinitely more. If Adam's fall is drastic and far-reaching, *how much more* is Christ's so great redemption and deliverance when He took us not only to death and the grave but also raised us up with Him to the spiritual level. (Notice the *blue broken* line with its upward trend.) Remember that burial is not the end. The gospel delivered unto us is that Christ died *and rose*. "We were buried therefore with him through baptism into death: that. . . *we also might walk in newness of life*" (Rom. 6:4). Christ did not remain in the grave, for God raised His Son from the dead on the third day. But since His Son had become identified with man, at His resurrection He raised up a new creation with Him, making it to "sit with him in the heavenly places, in Christ Jesus" (Eph. 2:6). For "*if* we have become united with him in the likeness of his death, *we shall be* also in the likeness of his resurrection" (Rom. 6:5). "If any man is in Christ, he is a new creature: the old things are passed away; behold, they are become new" (II Cor. 5:17).

By birth man is unregenerate or natural. But on the basis of being identified with Jesus both in His death and in His resurrection, man *can* by faith become spiritual. (Study the chart to clarify this possibility.) Adam before the Fall and Jesus Christ while on earth lived sinless lives. Today we too can become spiritual and live on earth free from sin on the basis of Christ's redemption. "Made free from sin, ye became servants of righteousness" (Rom. 6:6, 18, 22).

This new life is by faith. As we received Christ initially by faith, so now we are to walk by faith. This does not mean that it is not real. *It is more real* than the things that are seen, "for the things which are seen are temporal; but the things which are not seen are eternal" (II Cor. 4:18). Therefore "as. . . ye received Christ Jesus the Lord, so walk in him" (Col. 2:6).

This spiritual level, however, is not a state of grace from which we *cannot fall* (though it is one from which we *need not fall*). To be spiritual is to be rightly related to Christ; it is to walk and be led by the Spirit of God. "As many as are led by the Spirit of God, these are sons of God" (Rom. 8:14). Certainly the Spirit of God will not lead us into sin; He will lead us into holiness. If we will but respond to the leading of the Spirit, we will walk even as He walked (I John 2:6) and be holy as He is holy, and so pass the test of being a child of God.

Of course, all outside of Christ live on the carnal level (which is the same as the sin and flesh level). But many who claim to be Christians are also walking on this level. Paul had to write to the Corinthians: "I . . . could not speak unto you as unto *spiritual*, but as unto *carnal*, as unto *babes in Christ*." Thus, in spite of redemption, it is possible to live on the carnal level, for man still has his own free will to choose self or Christ. Redemption must be individually appropriated. A man living on the carnal level *by choice* is not saved. The salvation of a man who lives on the carnal level *through ignorance* is dependent upon faith in Christ and full obedience to the light which he has. He who refuses to surrender fully to Christ is rejecting and despising the provision God has made for his full salvation. He is trampling under foot the blood of Christ that was poured out for him. "A man that hath set at nought Moses' law dieth without compassion on the word of two or three witnesses: of *how much sorer punishment*, think ye, *shall he be judged worthy*, who hath trodden under foot the Son of God, and hath counted the blood of the covenant wherewith he was sanctified an unholy thing, and hath done despite unto the Spirit of grace?" (Heb. 10:28, 29).

Many seem to think that Christ's power of full redemption is much less than the consequences of Adam's fall, but in Romans 5 we are told five times that the power of Christ's redemption is *much more* than the consequences of the Fall. There is *super-abundance of grace!* There is enough grace not only for the forgiveness of sins and to get man somehow into heaven, but *enough grace for a victorious life*, for a life that will fully please God. "If, by the trespass of one, death reigned through the one; *much more* shall they that receive the abundance of grace and of the gift of righteousness reign in life through the one, even Jesus Christ" (Rom. 5:12, 17). Rejoice in all such promises.

Long before creation, man's redemption in the person of God's Son was planned, and when the fullness of time came, it was executed and became history. On the basis of that redemption, God's power is now able to save and to restore us to the life which God planned for us.

Enoch, who lived long before the Cross became history, is an example of walking on the spiritual level. By faith he so looked forward to the Cross and laid hold of the grace and power of God that he was transformed and had witness borne to him that he was *well-pleasing unto God*. Hebrews 11:5, 6 says,

"By faith Enoch was translated that he should not see death; and he was not found, because God translated him: for he hath had witness borne to him that before his translation he had been well-pleasing unto God: and without faith it is impossible to be well-pleasing unto him; for he that cometh to God must believe that he is, and that he is a rewarder of them that seek after him."

But a walk on the spiritual level is not possible today, many say. Such people have been trying to live the victorious life *in their own strength*. To live our lives as best we can after we have believed in Christ and accepted Him as our Saviour is not enough. Most Christians agree to this, but they differ concerning *how much God can do*. But redemption is complete! And if God does *not* transform a sinner into a saint in walk as well as in his standing, it is because of rebellion or pride! A man's refusal to let God have His full way with him is rebellion! And if a man does not believe that God can save him completely, he is saying that God has finally found a problem He cannot solve. This reasoning is pride of the worst form, for it is making self bigger than God!

With a man who is fully surrendered to Him, God can do anything He pleases. What is needed is that we come to Christ and admit that we cannot *of ourselves* live the Christian life any more than we could save ourselves. That is why Jesus made so plain to us His terms of discipleship: "If any man would come after me, let him *deny himself*, and take up his cross, and follow me" (Matt. 16:24). We must *deny* ourselves; we must *give up* all our rights; we must *surrender* ourselves fully into the hands of God. "Whosoever he be of you that *renounceth* not all that he hath, he cannot be my disciple" (Luke 14:33). We must *forsake* all, or we cannot be His disciples! We must trust Him fully and only. In no other way can God free us from dependence upon ourselves or things. If we will trust Him, the Holy Spirit will reproduce in us the life of Jesus Christ and enable us to walk as He walked.

Some say that they cannot understand how we can walk as He walked. No, friends, it cannot be understood any more than the initial crisis of salvation can be understood by the natural mind. It must be experienced to be understood. Let us not then come short of God's eternal purpose for man. God said, "Let us make man in our image, after our likeness." "Ye shall be holy, for I am holy." He is "able to do exceeding abundantly above all that we ask or think, according to the power that worketh in us, unto him be the glory in the church and in Christ Jesus unto all generations for ever and ever. Amen."

CHAPTER SIX

"TEMPTATION ... SUCH AS MAN CAN BEAR"

> "Count it all joy, my brethren, when
> ye fall into manifold temptations;
> knowing that the proving of your faith
> worketh patience. And let patience
> have its perfect work, that ye may be
> perfect and entire, lacking in nothing"
> (James 1:2–4).

TEMPTATION," says Luther, "is one of the three things needed for a saint's development." If this be true, and it certainly is, temptation must not be viewed as an altogether evil thing, having no good purpose whatever. Temptation has a definite purpose, for in infinite wisdom God left His redeemed children temptable and tempted. That definite purpose, according to James 1:3, is the proving of our faith. We must therefore face the fact that every temptation is meant by God to be a means of grace, an opportunity to prove to God that we love Him supremely. He has made us willing, choosing, loving beings. He longs for us to express and prove our faith and love for Him when we are not only capable of self-love, but even when we are living in an environment where there is much opportunity for self-seeking. God does not want us to be

79

automatons, forced into loving and serving Him; He wants us to love Him because we want to.

A little illustration may help to show us these things (even though it is totally inadequate when applied to our Father in heaven). Pastors, evangelists, and other workers for God often find it necessary to be away from home for periods of time. On their return there is a spontaneous expression of joy and love from the family —especially if the separation has been for a long time. But suppose the returning father, who finds himself almost embraced to death by his little children, asks, "Why do you cling to me so?" and then receives the answer, "Because we have to and because it is our duty." Don't you see how the joy and gladness of his heart would depart? Yet, though keenly disappointed, the earthly father would seek in some other way to cause his children to want to love him.

Even so, our heavenly Father has always been doing everything He can to win our love. Though He has allowed temptations, these have been giving us ample opportunities to prove our love for Him. Viewed in this way, temptation is not something to flee from, always one step behind us, ready at any moment to overtake us, but temptation is something to be overcome. In its fiercest hour and in every opportunity in which we *could* do the very opposite, God wants us to win a positive victory by *choosing Him* and *His* will. In this way it *is* possible to count temptation all joy and thus enter into the inheritance promised from the Word to the man that endureth temptation: "For when he hath been approved, he shall receive the crown of life, which the Lord promised to them that love him" (James 1:12).

As we continue to study in detail this subject of temptation, we shall confine ourselves chiefly to the Christian's temptations (though one who is *not* saved may also find truths that may be helpful in seeking and understanding the life offered by our Lord Jesus Christ). Thoroughly converted Christians need special instruction on this subject because again and again they yield to temptation through a lack of understanding of the essential factors in temptation. That our crafty, wily foe, Satan (who knows exactly where to strike), may have no ground to work on in us, let us carefully examine three major aspects on this subject of temptation. Let us study Adam and Eve's temptation along three lines: the devil's method of attack on Adam and Eve; the responses which the tempted ones gave to the devil's suggestions; and finally, how to overcome in the hour of temptation.

In the Garden of Eden, Adam and Eve did not have any lack either in their endowment or their environment. Though they had no sinful nature, yet in God's infinite wisdom they were allowed to face the intrusion of Satan and temptation. We are mistaken, therefore, if we think that in a soul cleansed from indwelling sin there is nothing for the devil to tempt. Before the Fall Adam and Eve were tempted, even though neither of them had any sin. Conditions in the Garden of Eden were more ideal than they have ever been since; yet even so they were temptable. (So was Jesus Christ, the last Adam, temptable.) Not only *could* Adam and Eve sin; they *did* sin. Nor must we confuse temptation with sin, or let Satan, the accuser of the brethren, weigh us down with false condemnation. It is not sin to be tempted, for we are told that Christ was tempted on every point, yet He did not sin.

In Genesis 3 we see Satan busy tempting two souls through a serpent, the pre-Fall serpent, who was no doubt an erect and beautiful creature. Why Adam was not on his guard when he found this animal talking, we are not told. Surely the strangeness of an animal talking should have been enough to warn him. In addition, it was clear that God intended Adam to refer all things to Him and never to strike off in independent action. For Adam was not omniscient, even though he possessed a degree of intelligence far above that of anyone born since the Fall. Yet Adam's understanding and knowledge were limited, for the very name of the tree from which he ate, called the tree of the knowledge of good and evil, would seem to indicate this.

What then are Satan's ways, both in the Garden of Eden and to this present day? The enemy of our souls, the father of lies, attacked our first parents by means of two lies, insinuating one and asserting the other. The first lie, which the devil only insinuated, was this: *"Yea, hath God said, Ye shall not eat of any tree of the garden?"* There is a subtle insinuation in this question. We miss the main point if we see only Satan's raising this question, for he was lying and seemed to be saying, "God does not love you, Adam and Eve. God isn't fair. If He really loved you, He would not put restrictions upon you or deny you the pleasure of eating the fruit of this beautiful tree. Is God as mean as all that? Surely you understand that He does not love you, or you would be free to do everything you pleased."

Today the devil is still a liar and the father of lies. He approaches man as he did thousands of years ago and tells him that God does not really love him. He knows that if we are absolutely convinced God loves us and is concerned about us and is seeking only our highest good, we can bear anything. But if we believe this insinuated lie, then discouragement, depression, self-pity, despair, and countless other sins occur. Through believing the devil's lies, men remain defeated, weak, sick, and unable to lay hold of God's promises that are repeated over and over again in Scripture. But what a difference it makes to be thoroughly convinced that God does love all men! Jesus said, "Ye shall *know the truth,* and the truth shall make you free" (John 8:32). One of these truths told over and over again in Scripture is that *God does love us,* for God is love (I John 4:16). "He is an eternal will to all goodness!" He showers forth His love upon all, the bad as well as the good. Eve should have known and did know this, but was temporarily caught off balance. Even though she had not yet taken the plunge, she was already being tempted, and beginning to respond to temptation.

Satan's second lie to Adam and Eve was a direct one: "Ye shall *not* surely die" (Gen. 3:4). He did not insinuate now, but dared to make a statement which was the direct opposite to what God had said:

"Ye *shall* surely die" (Gen. 2:17). He did not dare to start out with a direct lie; but now that he had their attention and his questions were already in their minds. he dared to contradict the spoken word of God.

This second lie is deeper and more dangerous than the first. It is saying, "You can sin and get by with it. Disobedience will not result in death. Punishment is delayed, so you will escape. You can sin and not suffer the consequences." No wonder men today are bold in their sin. No wonder there is no conviction for sin. If men in our day knew that their sin would be followed by inevitable consequences, how many would dare sin? Truly the devil is the father of such false hopes. How often today the devil tries and succeeds in the very same thing. not only with sinners but also with Christians. What else but Satan's lies can be the cause of today's carnality, selfishness, and low level of Christian living? We are in danger of being so un-balanced in the matter of grace that we actually use it as a license to sin; in fact, some have such a light view of sin that they believe God wills for sin to continue in a Christian in order to keep him humble. But Jesus is the Saviour from sin as well as from hell. Even after we have fallen into sin, He who saved us is certainly able to cleanse us. He is also able to keep us from fall-ing if only we will refuse to believe the devil and his lies, and rather believe God's truth that "if the Son shall make you free, ye shall be free indeed."

We have just considered the line of the devil's direct attack. Next, let us see the gradual response from the ones attacked. "When the woman saw that the tree was *good for food,* and that it was a *delight to the eyes,* and that the tree was to be *desired to make one wise,* she took of the fruit thereof, and did eat; and she gave also unto her husband with her, and he did eat" (Gen. 3:6). Here we learn the temptability of man: the tree was "good for food," "a delight to the eyes," and "to be desired to make one wise." The Apostle John calls these "the lust of the flesh," "the lust of the eyes," and "the vain-glory of life" (I John 2:16).

To be tempted, man does not need to have a sinful nature; in fact, he is not tempted through a sinful nature, for that is not the object of the devil's attack. Man is tempted through his natural desires. These are not wrong in themselves, for they are God-given, and so are for man's good. But through wrong use, man's desires may become abnormal and defiled, especially if the wrong use is habitual. Yet if properly controlled, these desires may remain pure and good.

In the divine record of the first human temptation, these three fundamental desires are clearly indicated. First of all, there is a natural *desire to enjoy things.* The Word says Eve saw that "the tree was good for food." Here is a natural desire for the things of the body—for food, sleep, sex, etc. These are not wrong in themselves but must not be misused. The second is the *desire to get things* and is indicated by the words "the tree was a delight to the eyes." This brings to one's attention things outside oneself that he could get for himself in one way or another. The desire is not wrong in itself but may lead to something wrong by trying to get it in the wrong way, or else by getting more than God wants one to have. The third desire, *to do things*, is referred to by the words "the tree was to be desired to make one wise." This is the desire to accomplish things for self, for the world, or for God. Here, too, this desire is not essentially wrong but may lead to pride if we seek to accomplish more than God has led us to do.

Christ's temptation by the devil, as recorded in Luke 4:1–13, follows the same pattern. He attacked Christ on these same three points:

First—To enjoy things ("the lust of the flesh")

"If thou art the Son of God, command this stone that it become bread."

Second—To get things ("the lust of the eyes")

"He led him up, and showed him all the kingdoms of the world in a moment of time. And the devil said unto him, To thee will I give all this authority, and the glory of them: For it hath been delivered unto me; and to whomsoever I will give it. If thou therefore wilt worship before me, it shall all be thine."

Third—To do things ("the vain glory of life")

"He led him to Jerusalem, and set him on the pinnacle of the temple, and said unto him, If thou art the Son of God, cast thyself down from hence: for it is written, He shall give his angels charge concerning thee, to guard thee: and, on their hands shall they bear thee up, lest haply thou dash thy foot against a stone."

Regarding Christ's temptation, we are told in Hebrews that He was one "that hath been in all points tempted like as we are, yet without sin" (4:15). We conclude, therefore, that Christ's threefold temptation was a total temptation. It took in all points of man's nature, not necessarily tempting him with every individual sin possible for man to commit, but tempting Him on every single point or every side of his nature (including body, soul, and spirit). This is a total temptation.

Jesus Christ had these same three desires, and the enemy of our souls tried to cause Him to fail both as a man and as a Saviour by leading Him to satisfy His desires in a wrong way and at the wrong time. The devil's suggestion that He make bread out of stones, of course, was addressed to the desires of His body *to enjoy things;* his suggestion that He fall down and worship him as the price of receiving the kingdoms of the world was addressed to Christ's natural desire *to get things.* Surely He came to get the kingdoms of the world, and He *will* get them some day, but not in a wrong way. This was the devil's suggestion that He side-step Calvary. This temptation, as well as the first, was refused. The last suggestion was that He jump off the pinnacle of the temple and thus not only do the miraculous, but do the miraculous in such a way that the Jews might receive Him as the Messiah. This was an appeal to His natural desire *to do things.*

The devil therefore seeks entrance through one or all of these three natural, fundamental desires—to enjoy things, to get things, and to do things. Dr. Kyle's definition of temptation is rather difficult to improve upon: "Temptation is the incitement of our natural desires to go beyond the bounds set by God." We are tempted by Satan along the lines of our human desires. The devil does not tempt a sinful nature;

there is no point in tempting evil with evil. In our case, human nature is a *fallen* nature, but not in the experience of Adam and Eve, nor of Christ (for they had no *fallen* nature). They did have a *human* nature which was temptable, for it had these three fundamental, natural desires which could respond to temptation. While man is temptable through these desires and can respond to the enticements or the allurements of the devil or the world, yet by the promise of Hebrews 2:18, "he is able to succor them that are tempted." Praise God for this truth!

To the devil's planned attack on their three fundamental desires, Eve and then Adam responded fully. They took the fatal plunge, for we read, "She took of the fruit thereof, and did eat; and she gave also unto her husband with her, and he did eat." The awful result of their fall was threefold: *God*-ward, it resulted in alienation from God, manifested in spiritual and physical death. *Self*-ward, its results were condemnation and corruption, and their inner nature defiled. *Satan*-ward, the Fall resulted in enslavement to a subtle, cruel, crafty foe who, having succeeded in causing their fall, sought to accomplish their destruction.

But praise God for the truth that our so great a salvation (accomplished for us by Christ on Calvary) meets man's three basic needs: *First*, God forgives the sins of all those who repent of their sins and believe on Jesus Christ our Substitute, who died in our stead. By receiving Him, we have eternal life and are reconciled to God. *Second*, through His blood and Cross He makes possible the cleansing and altering of our very nature so that we need no longer continue being defiled but may be cleansed and purified. We read that "the blood ... cleanseth us from *all* sin," and that God "cleansed their hearts by faith." *Third*, through the indwelling Spirit and His consequent power for daily life, He makes possible the deliverance from the power of the devil.

But God allows Satan to tempt the Christian. Therefore we are to conclude that there is a positive element in temptation. Temptation is allowed not for the purpose of causing our fall but rather to make us strong and to give us an opportunity to prove our absolute love and devotion to Christ (even though we are perfectly free to do the opposite). The Epistle of James gives a good exposition on temptation:

> "Blessed is the man that endureth temptation, for when he hath been approved, he shall receive the crown of life, which the Lord promised to them that love him. Let no man say when he is tempted, I am tempted of God; for God cannot be tempted with evil, and he himself tempteth no man: but each man is tempted, when he is drawn away by his own lust, and enticed. Then the lust, when it hath conceived, beareth sin: and the sin, when it is fullgrown, bringeth forth death. Be not deceived, my beloved brethren" (James 1:12–16).

Man is tempted "when he is drawn away *by his own lust*, and enticed." Usually we attach a bad meaning to the word *lust*, though strictly speaking, it means nothing more than *a strong desire*. The meaning of the Greek word lust is to "set the heart upon, to long for" (rightfully or otherwise). This is where the battle is joined. It is in his desires that the man is enticed.

Only when lust has conceived does it bring forth. Until the will marries the wrong desire, there is no conception. Unless the will yields to the enticement, there is no sin. Only when the will yields to the desire is there a conception and sin; the child of lust is born. Someone has said, "Temptation begins with a simple evil thought; the next step is a strong imagination; then, a delight; and finally, a consent to the thing itself." Only when the thought reaches the point of consent is it sin. (These four stages may all occur in the mind without an outward act.) It is necessary, however, to deal with the suggestion at the very first before it becomes easier to yield or consent to it. The whole tone of the Word of God is that we be saved and kept from sinning in order that we might delight the heart of Jesus by doing His works. "We are his workmanship, created in Christ Jesus for good works, which God afore prepared that we should walk in them." Indeed, "if any man sin, we have an Advocate with the Father, Jesus Christ the righteous" (I John 2:1). Note here that it does not say *when* we sin, but it says *if* we sin. *If it so happens that we sin,* God in His mercy has made provision whereby we can come back to Him, confessing our sin. He will forgive and restore us again to that fellowship we enjoyed before the sin occurred. This ought to be done instantly, for as soon as we are conscious of sin or failure of any kind, we ought to flee to Christ, confessing all, and thus enjoy His constant fellowship. This is what it means to walk in the light.

Have you ever noticed the great passage on temptation in I Corinthians 10:13, "There hath no temptation taken you but such as man can bear: but God is faithful, who will not suffer you to be tempted above that ye are able; but will with the temptation make also the way of escape, that ye may be able to endure it"? This promise is placed between two warnings: The first, "Let him that thinketh he standeth take heed lest he fall"; and the second, "Wherefore, my beloved, flee from idolatry." This proves that God holds forth the possibility of absolute victory in every circumstance, and His own Word tells us that we will never be tempted above that we are able. But at the same time, God exhorts us to be eternally vigilant to keep our desires under the control of the Holy Spirit, not letting them strike out for themselves, not letting them clamor to the point where we yield our will to what we know of a surety is not God's plan for us. Remember, every temptation is a means of grace and a real opportunity to prove to God that we love Him supremely. In this way we are approved, and shall receive "the crown of life, which the Lord promised to them that love him."

CHAPTER SEVEN

DOES A CHRISTIAN HAVE TWO NATURES?

> "Our old man was crucified with him,
> that the body of sin might be *done
> away*, that so we should no longer be
> in bondage to sin" (Romans 6:6).

MANY a Christian thinks that to be thoroughly orthodox he must believe that not only every sinner but also every Christian *has* a sinful nature. Therefore, regardless of his spiritual progress, he must carry this sinful nature with him as long as he lives. It logically follows that he believes release from this inward enemy comes at death; and so in this way he identifies his sinful nature with his physical body. Perhaps this is not exactly what he believes, but since he is holding the wrong premise from the beginning, it is the only logical conclusion he can reach. (The meaning of the word "nature," especially as used in theology, is foreign to the Scriptures. There, the word does not often occur, and when it does, nature refers to what we do naturally.)

The general idea in the minds of many believers, then, is something like this: a sinner already *has* a sinful nature; when that sinner is saved, he receives a new nature (this makes two natures plus his humanity); he is also a partaker of the divine nature which is Christ (this makes four); and in addition, such a one is sometimes influenced by the devil. Therefore, in or about the believer are five natures! Can this be possible? No! It is altogether too complicated and utterly ridiculous. He has arrived at the wrong conclusion by thinking of man as *having* a sinful nature. Herein is one of the main errors in Christendom. If in his thinking he begins wrong, then all his conclusions will be also wrong. The wrong idea about man's sinfulness and man's nature limits a Christian's experience and fruitfulness.

A sinner, then, does not *have* a sinful nature; he *is* sinful. We all see the difference, I trust, between *having* something bad and *being* something bad. If it were just a matter of *having* an evil nature, then it would be almost the same as saying, "*I'm* all right: but this thing I inherited from my father Adam, and that I carry about with me, is sinful." To such reasoners, the only hope seems to be either to have this sinful nature extracted, or finally at the end of the earthly life to lay this evil intruder aside in death. The whole trouble with this attempt at a solution to the question is that on the one hand it is impossible to have one's nature (the real you) extracted; and, on the other hand, not many of us are willing to die just yet. On the contrary, we want to live, and we want to live in Christian victory and fruitfulness.

Many have the idea that belief in two natures is synonymous with orthodoxy. But a careful search of the Scriptures will give no support to the idea of man's nature as a separate entity. Man is a unitary being. If not, he is a schizophrenic! Neither of the two main passages which deal with inner conflicts (Romans 7 and Galatians 5:16–26) mentions the word *nature*. The reason for this is that Paul is not describing a person with two natures (one good and one bad) which must co-exist until the grave. He is speaking of a person who must make a definite choice to walk either "in the Spirit" or else "after the flesh." The prince of Bible commentators, G. Campbell Morgan, says, "I most certainly do not believe that man ever has two natures at once. I believe he has one nature always, and that conversion is its cleansing and renewal." The prince of revivalists, Charles G. Finney, would have nothing to do with the prevalent idea of an inherited sinful nature as a separate entity, a punishment for Adam's sin, infused into the whole race of fallen man. Such an idea, Finney believed and proved, really provided an excuse for sin. Mr. Finney says, "The fact that Christ died in man's stead and on behalf of sinners proves that God regarded man not as unfortunate but as criminal, and altogether without excuse. Surely Christ need not have died to atone for the *misfortunes* of men. His death was to atone for their *guilt*." Sin or sinfulness is a crime; God holds us responsible for it. Therefore, we cannot hide under the smoke screen either of the old man, or a *sinful* nature, or a *duality* of natures. Man in his unregenerate state does not *have* a sinful nature—he *is* sinful; he *is* responsible; he *is* a criminal.

If Ambrose (340-397) introduced the idea of a *sinful* nature, it was Augustine (354–430) who developed the idea of the believer's *two* natures and introduced it as a respectable doctrine of Christianity. Careful study of this subject, however, will prove that Augustine found the two-natures idea not in the Bible but in his own past experience in Manichaeism. Ever since Augustine carried over the dualistic philosophy from Manichaeism and brought it into the Christian Church, it has been the Church's plague. It is probably true that the Scriptures were never studied as carefully in the original languages as at the time of the Reformation. However, it is most unfortunate that for the development of the doctrine of sin and sinfulness neither Luther nor Calvin went back to the apostolic writings alone but accepted the teaching of Augustine without question. The reformers presented the idea that original sin was guilt, and that sinfulness and inability to do right (a fettered will) is the penalty of sin, and therefore passed on to all of Adam's progeny. Such a view makes sinfulness a calamity and not a crime—a misfortune or disease for which man (except Adam) is not responsible. But this is not Scriptural, for everywhere God does hold man responsible, commanding him to repent. In unmistakable terms God states that unless a man will repent and receive the provision for his forgiveness and regeneration through the atonement of Jesus Christ, he will suffer eternal consequences for sins committed.

The teaching of the two natures, and especially of a sinful nature as a separate entity which a man inherits from his father Adam, only confuses the issue and produces an excuse for sinning. The real issue, the choice between self and Christ, has shifted to a conflict between two natures both indwelling the same person. Augustine, before his controversy with Pelagius, taught that a man could live a holy life *with* the help of God. The heresy of his opponent caused him to take the extreme position that even with the help of God man could *not* live a holy life. After meeting Augustine, Pelagius (360–420 A.D.) also took the extreme position that a man could live a holy life *without* the help of God. He did this because Christians, even the clergy, were excusing their sinfulness by blaming this separate entity of a sinful nature. Augustine, as we said before, believed in the continuing sinful nature. As a result, he had no hope of purity of heart. He believed in no deliverance—at least after meeting Pelagius, that was his final conclusion. He considered pleasure in the taking of food a sin, saying, "This much hast Thou [God] taught me that I should bring myself to take food as a medicine." He considered love for music a sin. It was also a sin to him for the eyes "to delight in fair and varied forms and pleasing bright colors." He considered it a sin to watch a hound chase a rabbit, or to gaze at a lizard and a spider catching flies, because these actions would be prompted by curiosity, which is always evil, according to his theology.

As Christians today we must guard against thinking of a special sinful nature imposed upon man after sinning; we must also guard against the idea of a constitutional sinfulness—that is, locating sin in the physical body. The first would make us a split personality, and the second would give no hope for deliverance until physical death.

But what is sin? Sin is a transgression of the law; sin is disobedience; sin is selfishness (a preference of self to God); sin is a crime. Adam's sin caused immediate spiritual death, but it caused more than that. Adam's body was weakened (he became subject to physical death); his mind was impaired; his emotions, being disturbed, were no longer in harmony. That we are all involved in Adam's sin (original sin) the Bible makes unmistakably clear in Romans 5:12. So then no one is born into this world as Adam was (before the Fall), for all inherit depravity, the result of Adam's sin. I do not think anyone would argue against the fact that a weakened body, an impaired mind, and disturbed emotions are common to everyone. This, however, is not guilt. Nor would it be right to call it moral depravity since on our part it involves no choice of will. However, the Bible makes unmistakably clear the fact that everyone *becomes* morally depraved—that is, everyone chooses sin. In fact, a child is committed to selfishness long before reason is developed. Then when reason is developed, he continues in the same direction and makes the same choice as Adam. He makes the wrong choice right at the beginning and very early in life, for he lives in an anti-Christ and pro-self world. Not having a perfect body, a perfect mind, or perfect emotions—surrounded by an almost universal example of selfishness, and tempted by the devil—man falls prey to sin on his own. Thus, as a voluntary transgressor and as a morally depraved creature, he is subject to punishment—eternal banishment from the presence of God. His only hope is to repent, to be forgiven, and then believe in the provision that God has made for his salvation and deliverance—namely, the atonement of Jesus Christ on Calvary.

We see, therefore, that both the Scriptures and Christian experience teach that the natural man *is* sinful. He is not only partly wrong but all wrong. This is because of two things: his relationship to fallen Adam and his choice. Not only is his human nature (his whole being) polluted, but he is a voluntary transgressor. Some are more skillful in concealing this sinfulness, but under favorable circumstances (or shall we say unfavorable) definite acts of sin reveal the truth.

Originally, man was created in the image of God with a blessed prospect of continuing in that image and of being indwelt by his Creator. As long as he continued in this state, his nature was pure and his acts were above reproach. But there came a time (described in Genesis 3) when man's relationship to his God came to an end and when he became *related to another*, even the devil. While in proper relationship to God, his nature was pure; but now, related to the devil, his nature is defiled.

One of the best descriptions of this change of relationship which took place at the Fall is in connection with the Gerasene demoniac who had an unclean spirit and was possessed with demons (Mark 5). At that time no man could bind him. He was crying out continually and cutting himself with stones. But after being delivered from his wrong relationship to the devil and having entered into a right relationship to Christ, he that had been possessed with demons was now "clothed and in his right mind" and filled with one desire—to be with his Lord.

So this is not a matter of a nature to be removed or extracted but rather a matter of relationships. To whom are we related? Related to the devil we are polluted; but related properly to Christ we are made pure. Though we need *forgiveness* for what we sinners have done, yet for what we are, we need *cleansing*. Our nature is not to be discarded but cleansed—cleansed from *all* unrighteousness (I John 1:9). Christ can change the foulest sinner and make him pure and spotless. To Christians the promise is not only that we are delivered from the devil's kingdom and placed into Christ's kingdom (according to Colossians 1:13), but that through the deliverance, by accepting death to self through the Cross, we can be *thoroughly* and *completely changed*. Christ delivers us *out of* the power of darkness and translates us *into* the kingdom of the Son of His love.

This truth is also made plain in Christ's parable of the vine and the branches (John 15). The very fact that Jesus calls himself the *true* Vine implies that there is a *false* vine, which, of course, is Satan. All men are drawing their life either from the true or the false vine—either from Jesus Christ or from Satan.

The fall of our first parents is also illustrated clearly in the parable of Isaiah 5:1-7. This passage, referring primarily to Israel, also gives a true picture of fallen man.

> "A song of my beloved touching his vineyard. My well-beloved had a vineyard in a very fruitful hill: and he digged it, and gathered out the stones thereof, and planted it with the choicest vine, and built a tower in the midst of it, and also hewed out a winepress therein: and he looked that it should bring forth grapes, and it brought forth wild grapes. And now, . . . judge,

... betwixt me and my vineyard. What could have been done more to my vineyard, that I have not done in it? wherefore, when I looked that it should bring forth grapes, brought it forth wild grapes?"

This very fruitful hill could represent the Garden of Eden. Conditions there were so absolutely ideal that God could truly say, "What could have been done more to my vineyard that I have not done in it?" Yet our first parents did *not* bring forth sweet grapes as expected but only wild grapes. The quality of their fruit is described in Deuteronomy 32:32, 33: "Their vine is of the vine of Sodom, and of the fields of Gomorrah: their grapes are grapes of gall, their clusters are bitter: their wine is the poison of serpents, and the cruel venom of asps."

Let us then see exactly what happened to man at the Fall. First, he *turned away from God;* second, he *turned to another*, even Satan. But, likewise, on Calvary Jesus Christ did two things: first, He destroyed the power of the false vine (Satan) and made it possible for anyone "in Satan" to renounce his allegiance and relationship to Satan; second, in His suffering and death He opened up His own heart and made it possible for anyone who would renounce the devil and his claims to be grafted into Him, the True Vine.

Man is so constituted that he can not exist alone but must be related to either Satan or Christ. Though originally his human nature was indwelt by God, by his Fall he forfeited this divine indwelling. In its place he received the life of the enemy of our souls, Satan; for by nature, says God, we were the children of wrath

(Eph. 2:3). "Ye are of your father the devil," said Jesus, "and the lusts of your father it is your will to do" (John 8:44).

Because we all partake of the nature of one of these two vines, we all bring forth fruit according to that nature, for "do men gather grapes of thorns, or figs of thistles? Even so every good tree bringeth forth good fruit; but the corrupt tree bringeth forth evil fruit. A good tree cannot bring forth evil fruit, neither can a corrupt tree bring forth good fruit . . . . By their fruits ye shall know them" (Matt. 7:16–20). But it is not possible for a branch to remove *itself* from the devil's vine and be placed into the True Vine, Christ. Every natural branch taken from one tree and grafted into another *must* have the help of the gardener's hand. Even so, all spiritual grafting must be done by another's hand. Salvation, then, is a work of God, a free gift through the redemption of Jesus Christ our Saviour. To be saved really means that a man is willing to forsake the false vine (with Satan as his father) and be grafted into the True Vine (with God as his Father). To be a Christian is not only to know or believe something. To be a Christian is a definite experience wherein one renounces his own life and then trusts in Christ and His finished work. For anyone who is willing thus to renounce the devil and all sin and who chooses to be grafted into Christ, the Holy Spirit will perform the necessary grafting, delivering him out of the false vine, Satan, and grafting him into the True Vine, Christ.

In Nature, when grafting takes place, the branch always bears fruit according to the tree from which it has been taken. But in spiritual experience, by going through the Cross a miracle takes place, and the branch begins to bear fruit according to the stock into which it is placed. We therefore see the absolute necessity of a real experience of crucifixion, else one will continue to bear the old fruit of the self-life. This explains the carnality in the church. So many have gone *around* the Cross instead of *through* the Cross in a real death to the self-life.

At the Fall, divine life went out and satanic life came in; in redemption, satanic life goes out and divine life comes in, for through God's precious and exceeding great promises we become "partakers of the divine nature, having *escaped* from the corruption that is in the world by lust" (II Pet.1:4).

Yet, even with Christ indwelling him, the born-again soul still has his own personal human nature with its appetites and desires. But we never have two natures—that is, two personal natures. All the way through, we have our human nature related either to the devil or to God. Thus, all who are grafted into Christ, whether babes or mature souls, partake of Christ's nature, for "he that is joined unto the Lord is *one* spirit" (I Cor. 6:17).

However, full consciousness of what is ours (by virtue of our having been delivered *from* the false vine and having been grafted *into* the True Vine) does not dawn upon us all at once. Then too, just after the transfer from the false to the True Vine, there may be sour sap (termed the self-life) still in the branch. But as surely as the branch grafted into the vine draws its sap from the new source, so surely will the upsurge of the life of Christ drive out all the sour sap that may have been in the branch. A full consciousness of what we have in Christ, a complete reliance on Him, and a receiving of the upsurge of the new life—all these will bring about the crisis of sanctification. And sanctification is not only a proper relationship to Christ but identification with Him *in a full and complete union*. The result will be that "made free from sin and become servants to God, ye have your fruit unto sanctification" (Rom. 6:22).

We must not identify *sinful nature* with the body, nor think of it as something separate from ourselves. Rather, we must realize that our sinful nature is our human nature in *wrong* relationship to the devil, and thus polluted. With this *wrong* relationship broken and a *right* relationship with Christ fully restored, the sinful nature is changed (metamorphosed) and becomes pure (like the caterpillar turned into a beautiful butterfly). Rightly do we sing,

"Let the beauty of Jesus be seen in me,
    All His wondrous compassion and purity;
    O Thou Spirit divine, *all my nature refine*
    Till the beauty of Jesus be seen in me."

Some will ask, "Does this mean that we *can* not sin any more? If a Christian does *not* have a sinful nature, what would there be in him to tempt?" The answer is that our Lord had no sinful nature and He too was tempted (though He did not sin). As we have said previously, of course we can be tempted and of course we can sin. Adam, fresh from the hands of God, had no sinful nature, yet was tempted (and sinned). We are tempted through our natural appetites, not through a sinful nature. Our appetites are not sinful in themselves, for they have been given to us by God; but unless they are controlled by the Holy Spirit, they will become sinful. Just as a branch, even while grafted into a true vine needs the constant care of a gardener, so must we be cared for, guarded, guided by the Holy Spirit. We must deny any desire or craving for something not consistent with the Vine in which we abide. That the old man is not only crucified but dead and buried is positionally true for every Christian (Rom. 6:6). But if we are to realize this blessing in experience, we must individually appropriate it through faith and through surrender of self to the death of the Cross.

There is, however, an evident duality in man. This is not a duality of two natures within one person, but rather it is a duality of flesh and spirit. When God made the angels, He made them spirits without bodies (physical bodies). When He made animals, He made them bodies without spirits. But when He made man, He made him both body and spirit—flesh and spirit. This is what the Apostle speaks of in both Romans 7 and Galatians 5. The issue, not settled in Romans 7, brings forth Paul's statement of frustration. The best that *I myself* can do is given for us in Romans 7:25: "So then I of myself with the mind, indeed, serve the law of God; but with the flesh the law of sin." The best that God can do is given in Romans 8. Galatians 5 gives the proper solution and there the Apostle says, "They that are of Christ Jesus have crucified the flesh with the passions and the lusts thereof" (Gal. 5:24).

Therefore the issue is whether or not to walk according to the flesh or the Spirit. The Apostle Paul says that they that are of Christ Jesus have settled this matter, and have deposed the flesh as a ruling agent, choosing to walk according to the Spirit. Thus there need not be a constant battle. It can be a settled matter.

The word *flesh*, strictly speaking, is not always identified as something bad. Christ, *"in the days of his flesh, . . .* offered up prayers" (Heb. 5:7). Certainly in His case, the flesh had no bad connotation. The flesh is the physical life—human nature with the appetites and passions. The word *flesh* is used in a bad sense only when it has usurped the place of the Spirit and is in control of the life. This wrong position of control must come to an end, must yield to the Spirit, and must come under the sweet influence of the Vine and Husbandman. Christ, who "pleased not himself," (Rom. 15:3) now tells us to follow in His steps. He says to us that we ought to deny self, take up our cross daily, and follow Him. Therefore, to live with a mine of corruption within (as many wrongly think is necessary), with a continual consciousness of sin, is wrong. With the flesh properly related to the Spirit (as servant and not master), we can abide in Christ moment by moment—cleansed by Christ's blood, and thus made pure and holy.

And so, once again let us remind ourselves that the central truth of Scripture is *full union with Christ.* Everything leads up to this truth. Christ desires that we become fully conscious of what it means to be completely united to Him, and yielded to His sweet nature and influences. If, after we have become united to

Christ, we yield to sin (though we need not), it should be only a momentary thing, instantly confessed, and forgiven and cleansed. A Christian does *not* live in sin; the will to sin is gone. But "*if* any man sin, we have an Advocate with the Father, Jesus Christ the righteous." "*If* we confess our sins, he is faithful and righteous to forgive us our sins, and to cleanse us from all unrighteousness."

CHAPTER EIGHT

SINLESS PERFECTION?

"Now the God of peace ... *make you perfect* in every good thing to do his will, working in us that which is *well-pleasing* in his sight, through Jesus Christ" (Hebrews 13:20, 21).

DOES the Bible teach sinless perfection in the passage just quoted from Hebrews (or in similar passages)? Almost everyone fears sinless perfection as he would a plague, though so many are indefinite as to exactly what the term means. In spite of its high-sounding name, to most Christians sinless perfection is the embodiment of all that is evil. Today a church will often tolerate a liar or a fornicator—both of whom are excluded from heaven—but one who believes in sinless perfection (rightly or wrongly we will discuss later) is at once accused of believing in a damnable heresy and dismissed.

Now every true Christian should so long for holiness (that is, Christ-likeness) that even if sinless perfection did not seem to be taught in Scriptures, the tendency should be to want to believe more rather than less of what is promised. In fact, it would seem commendable to put *more* value on the blood of Christ. Instead, we too often depreciate the atonement by saying that Christ's death on the Cross *does* bring peace into the heart and *will* get us to heaven somehow, but "we are only human, you know, and in this life must not expect too much."

The term sinless perfection is not found in the Bible. Because its definition is ambiguous, it really ought not to be used. Generally speaking, sinless perfection is used to mean a state in which the Christian *cannot sin*, a state where he is not only cleansed from all sin but freed from the temptation to sin, and therefore a state where the atonement is no longer needed. Such ideas are certainly not Scriptural, nor promised in the Word, nor necessary for living a victorious life. Aggressive souls are seeking a more perfect Christian experience, and critics certainly ought not to discourage such; therefore we all ought to be "pressing on" ourselves and be helping others to do the same.

The devil has coined this term, sinless perfection, and he uses it as a scare word, to scare away those seeking a holy life. So successful has he been in blinding minds and scaring hearts that few dare to make a personal investigation of the subject —preferring to put absolute reliance on what some-one else has said. Too often, unfortunately, these statements are not based on knowledge of what the Scriptures and others teach, but on what men think is being taught. We have a large library on the subject of sanctification (called by other names too, such as victorious life, holiness, Keswick teaching, etc.) and for many years have collected the best books on this subject. Yet in our wide reading, we have not found so much as one writer who used the term sinless perfection. Today we Christians have allowed the devil to have his way long enough. It is high time to expose him and to defeat his purpose.

Just here it may be well to ask ourselves a number of questions: Is there not a perfection which is Scriptural? Does not the Word of God promise Christian perfection? What has God promised to Christians? Is it possible to attain to the perfection of the triune God? Does God expect the Christian to be as perfect as the angels who have never known sin, and as perfect as Adam was before the Fall? What are the needs and longings of a true Christian? In answering these questions this much is plain: We are not angels; we are not God; we are not Adam before the Fall. We are sinners saved by grace and called Christians. And so, the perfection that God expects of us is this: to be by the grace of God (not by any strength or reason of our own) all that a Christian should be. This is Christian perfection.

On this subject, how we need clear thinking, a thinking based on the Word. From it we learn we are born not in the image of God but in the fallen image of Adam. More than that, we also learn from Scripture and from experience that every one born into the world *chooses* sin and thus becomes a voluntary transgressor. Not only does he commit acts of sin; he also resists the will of God and thus becomes a rebel. With some, this anarchy expresses itself in an open, outward way, while others seem to be more skillful in hiding their antagonism to the absolute authority of

God. But to us who are true Christians, there came a day when, deeply convicted, we repented of our sin, yielded to Christ, and were regenerated by the Holy Spirit. As we look back, we see the depths of sin from which we were saved. Our hearts and voices are lifted to God in praise for this wonderful grace of salvation.

But have you noticed that Hebrews 7:25 seems to pass over what we are saved *from* and makes mention only of what we are saved *to?* The Word says, "He is able to save *to the uttermost* them that draw near unto God through him, seeing he ever liveth to make intercession for them." It does not say *from* the uttermost; it says *to* the uttermost. There is an uttermost salvation which the true Christian longs for, aspires toward as an ideal, and, praise God, may possess in experience.

Again we ask the questions: "What is this *uttermost* salvation? What is Christian perfection?" Our Lord himself has something to say about perfection in Matthew 5:48: "Ye shall be *perfect*, as your heavenly Father is perfect." Is Jesus commanding something possible, or is He trying to drive us to despair? There *must* be a perfection that is possible, otherwise Christ would not have commanded it. Even an earthly father (much less our heavenly Father and His Son, Jesus Christ) would not command his children to do what he knows they cannot do. To find the perfection enjoined in verse 48, read the whole context of Matthew 5:44–48 carefully:

"I say unto you, Love your enemies, and pray for them that persecute you; that ye may be sons of your Father who is in heaven: for he maketh his sun to rise on the evil and the good, and sendeth rain on the just and the unjust. For if ye love them that love you, what reward have ye? do not even the publicans the same? And if you salute your brethren only, what do ye more than others? do not even the Gentiles the same? *Ye therefore shall be perfect, as your heavenly Father is perfect.*"

By nature we do not love our enemies; we love those who love us; we love especially those who do good to us. But here we read that the Father loves *all* and blesses *all*—not only the good and not only the just, but the evil and the unjust also. According to the context it is in love that we are to be perfect—not with a perfection of the head but of the heart. We are to have such love that we can love even our enemies and those who persecute us. Obviously this is not natural but divine love, the love of God himself, the love that God has "shed abroad in our hearts through the Holy Spirit" (Rom. 5:5). To the natural or carnal man this love is absolutely impossible. It is contrary to nature. But is it impossible for the spiritual man? No! Perfection of love is Christian perfection.

Turn to another passage where holiness is commanded: "Like as he who called you is holy, be ye yourselves holy in all manner of living; because it is written, *Ye shall be holy; for I am holy*" (I Pet. 1: 15, 16). For those who are not seeking the uttermost salvation, the ready answer (excuse) to this passage is that we are holy and perfect "in Christ." But Peter anticipated this excuse when he added a phrase after the word holy, whose meaning we cannot mistake: "holy *in all manner of living.*" In the King James Version it says "holy in all manner of conversation." This means that the whole expression of life should be one of practical holiness. We are not to be holy by proxy only. We are not to be perfect by proxy. We are to be holy right now and perfect in love right now. To stop at the truth of justification, which is only the beginning of what God wants to do for us, is a mistake. For Jesus' sake God justifies us *that He may make us just* and *holy*. The Bible teaches not only *imputation* of holiness, but also *impartation* of holiness, for it says, "We *are* partakers of the Holy Spirit (Heb. 6:4). Through His power He makes us what we ought to be.

So entirely contrary to our fallen nature is holiness that many think the needed change is beyond reach and possibility. It may be beyond a Christian's reach but not beyond God's. *Of course* this change from natural to divine love, from sinfulness to holiness, is beyond our human power. But thanks be to God, we are not left to our own feeble efforts in desiring the life that pleases God. If we meet the conditions, God will do what we cannot do. Most of us have the idea that we must sanctify ourselves and must make ourselves holy, not realizing that sanctification, as well as justification, is ours by faith. (I trust we are all orthodox enough to know that we cannot save ourselves.)

In Scripture this change that must take place if a believer is to be sanctified is called by different terms such as these: "transformed"; "crucified with Christ"; "one died for all, therefore all died"; "ye died"; "freed from sin"; "ceased from sin"; "our old man was crucified"; "dead unto sin but alive unto God";

"delivered"; "newness of life." All of these terms speak of a conclusive act and not just a process. One of the plainest of these passages is Colossians 1:13 where Paul under the inspiration of the Holy Spirit writes, "[He] delivered us out of the power of darkness, and translated us into the kingdom of the Son of his love." Here is not only deliverance from the power of darkness and placement into a new kingdom (the kingdom of Christ), but here also is implied a change wrought by God between these two kingdoms. It is here that we embrace the Cross in its delivering power. *We* can not do it; *we* can not attain to it by our own reason and strength. *But God can* transform and *does* transform those who trust Him.

Many of us think of sin (as well as sinfulness) as being identified with the human body, so that we believe sin must be retained until we close our eyes in physical death. But our human body is but the house in which we live. The real person is the spirit—something beyond the body which is but a member of the real person. Thus sin is not something material that must be extracted or eradicated, for it is deeper than the physical. Sin affects the soul and the body but does not have its seat in the body. Sin consists in a wrong relationship, in perversity, in depravity of free will, in the taint of selfishness, and is best described by Isaiah as wanting one's own way (Isa. 53:6).

But someone asks, "Can the nature of man really be changed? If so, where and how?" Yes, friends, the Bible teaches us that we can be changed, changed absolutely, changed entirely. It declares that when Jesus Christ went to the Cross, He not only suffered *for* our sins, taking them upon himself, but He did something more. *He also took the sinner himself to the Cross,* for the Word says, "One died for all, therefore all died" (II Cor. 5:14). Here is the change. It occurred almost two thousand years ago on Calvary. Positionally it is true for all of us. God believes it and declares it. It will also be true in a practical way if we will believe in the change. Over and over again, Romans 6 repeats that blessed truth that *we died* with Christ; *we are crucified* with Him; *we are buried* with Him. Therefore we must believe and obey His command to reckon ourselves dead to sin but alive unto God (Rom. 6:11). *Then* that blessed change will take place, and we *will* be transformed, translated, purged, and cleansed. Sin's reign *will* have ended; holiness *will* have begun.

So then, something need not be extracted from us (except sin), but rather our wrong relationship to the devil, to the world, and to self must end; a right relationship to God and His kingdom must begin. If we will submit to the Cross, we can experience this transforming work of the Holy Spirit. We must be willing to die to ourselves and to all our rights. Jesus said, "Whosoever doth not bear his own cross, and come after me, cannot be my disciple" (Luke 14:27). Our death to self must be as real an experience as His death was on Calvary. God alone can make us holy in life and perfect in love, but unless we make an entire, irrevocable surrender to Him in full consecration, even He *cannot* do this. Our will can stand in His way unless it is fully and forever yielded to Him who gave it. Only then can He carry out His own blessed work in us.

Let us not be satisfied with anything less than God's perfect work. Remember that "we are *his* workmanship, created in Christ Jesus for good works, which God afore prepared that we should walk in them" (Eph. 2:10). Our part is to yield our members to Him and to receive in faith that which He offers. Do you see, friends, that all is of God's grace? We were grateful to God for justification, were we not? Our hearts and voices should again be raised to God in deeper gratitude for His uttermost salvation. Having faith in our identification with Jesus Christ in His death and resurrection, let us rejoice much more in the *double* cure from sin's power and guilt.

But is the battle over? If we do yield fully to Christ and believe Him for His uttermost salvation, if we embrace the Cross in its fullest and deepest meaning, and if we allow the Holy Spirit to take us to the Cross so that we can reckon ourselves dead with Christ and raised with Him too—does this mean that we will not be tempted again? Does it mean that we *cannot* sin any more? Do we just wait for heaven? Not at all! On the contrary, it will mean that temptation will become more acute, and the battle will really begin. There will be work to be done, a fight to be fought, and the devil will contest our every step.

Moreover, it will never be enough just to know the facts of our redemption through the Cross of Calvary, nor even to have faith in the Cross and the deeper meaning of the Cross. There is more to follow. We must now begin to live a life consistent with our experience, a life of brokenness. We must actually manifest the lamb-like spirit of the Christ of the Cross. In place of the old spirit of retaliation, we must manifest the spirit of the Cross in true brokenness—always aware of what our sins cost Christ, as well as the possibility of still making mistakes and being re-ensnared by the devil (falling even deeper than ever before). Thus, ours must be a life lived in utter humility and in absolute dependence on Christ and His blessed Holy Spirit—our only desire being to please Christ in every thought, word and act.

Not only must our life be lived in brokenness, but also in perfect openness. We must now be willing to call sin, sin; we must be willing to admit our mistakes. No longer should we conceal our true thoughts. We must be willing to walk in the light, be judged by the light, be exposed and tried and tested on every point. If anything that is inconsistent with the holiness of Christ is revealed, we must confess it at once, put it away, and go to Jesus for cleansing again in the precious blood that makes us as spotless as the new fallen snow or the white wool of the mountain lamb. Having been made clean, we must then be kept clean.

Some erroneously think that professing the experience of Christ's uttermost salvation causes men to be careless about sin and to excuse sin. Nothing can be further from the truth. This experience makes a man's conscience more tender and more sensitive than ever. The tiniest smirch or spot, that would have been overlooked before, now feels as a weight, heavy as lead, and intolerable, causing one to flee afresh to Christ for cleansing, adjustment, instruction, or whatever may be needed. Praise God for the precious blood of Jesus

Christ, which not only cleanses once but continues its work of cleansing, and thus continually keeps all who trust in Him clean.

God's full desire for us is to touch others and overflow to them in His stead. We can be filled and running over continually as we are emptied of sin, selfness and worldliness, and clean through the blood of Christ (having received the Holy Spirit, first as a Person and then as an abiding Presence). This is what God expects. This is what God promises. This is what God has provided. This is the uttermost salvation which is all of grace and all of God—simply living out the life of Jesus by the power of the indwelling Spirit! What a wonderful salvation is ours!

CHAPTER NINE

CLEANSING THE TEMPLE

> "Your body is a temple of the Holy
> Spirit which is in you; . . . glorify God
> therefore in your body." "What agree-
> ment hath a temple of God with idols?
> for we are a temple of the living God"
> (I Cor. 6:19, 20 and II Cor. 6:16).

WE believe the miracles Jesus performed during
His public ministry were acted out parables and
therefore are deeply instructive. For instance, in His
first miracle, the changing of ordinary water into wine
in Cana of Galilee (John 2:1–11), He revealed himself as the Great Transformer with power to change a
yielded soul to conform to His own image.

According to John's Gospel, the second miracle took
place soon afterwards in the temple at Jerusalem (John
2:14–17). Jesus "found in the temple those that sold
oxen and sheep and doves, and the changers of money
sitting: and he made a scourge of cords, and cast all
out of the temple, both the sheep and oxen; and he
poured out the changers' money, and overthrew their
tables." More than natural power drove out the traders
and the money changers. At that same time, when
asked by the Jews to produce a sign showing His

authority, Jesus answered, "Destroy this temple, and in three days I will raise it up." Note He said *raise*, not *build* it up. Now the Jews, not understanding that He referred to His death and resurrection, reminded Him that Herod had been forty-six years in rebuilding and beautifying their temple. But Jesus was not thinking of Herod's temple, for "he spake of the temple of his body" (John 2:21). Until after the resurrection, even the disciples did not understand this.

This truth of the body as the temple of God is one of Christ's major revelations. As a boy He had called the temple in Jerusalem "my Father's house," the earthly house of the eternal and heavenly King. There God revealed himself, and there men communed with and worshipped Him. Even so, God has always wanted to make His home in His people and to live and walk in them. Isaiah, too, spoke of the high and lofty One who dwells not only in the high and holy place but *"with* him also that is of a contrite and humble spirit" (Isa. 57:15). The Apostle Paul attested further to this truth when he reminded the Corinthians, "Know ye not that your body is a temple of the Holy Spirit?" (I Cor. 6:19). The body of a Christian should be a shrine and home of God.

Jesus' miraculous cleansing of the temple in Jerusalem, then, is a most beautiful and instructive figure of the cleansing of the temple of our physical bodies. As we have already mentioned in chapter 7, the body had been considered for centuries to be the seat of evil and the chief hindrance to a holy life. Believing that we can not be free from sin until we are separated from our bodies, many have had only forlorn hope of deliverance from sin through physical death. This error of thinking of the body as the seat of sin was advanced very early in the Church's history. Even during the time of the apostles in the first century, Gnostics taught that matter was evil. The body, therefore, was sinful and only the spirit was good. To them, what a person did or permitted to be done in his body did not matter much, for the body was evil anyway. What happened to the body could not touch the spirit part of his being, they said. Of course the true servants of God vigorously opposed and rejected such an error.

However, three hundred years later, this teaching was again advanced, this time through Augustine. Before his conversion, Augustine was greatly influenced by Manichaeism, with its strong dualistic philosophy of nature and the association of evil with matter. While he may not have become a formal convert to the sect, he did hold their doctrines for several years. Of course he abandoned Manichaeism when he was converted to Christianity; however, traces of its teaching remained and were later incorporated into the doctrines of orthodox Christianity. The mixing of Christian truth and Manichaeian tendencies is revealed in Augustine's own words, for in one place he says, "Sin is nothing substantial, but a quality of the affections"; yet in another place he contradicts all this by saying that sin can only be "cured by the perfection of the sepulcher." This shows that Augustine and many following him believed that the body was the seat of sin.

However, in Christ's miracle of the cleansing of the temple, He showed that the body in itself is not evil. He reinstated a consecrated believer's body to its rightful place as a temple of the living God, as the element of man's being which ought to be presented to God as a holy and acceptable sacrifice. The truth is that the act of death has no sanctifying power, but right now we can be made free, we can be cleansed from all sin as by faith we appropriate Calvary's provision for our cleansing and our deliverance. How the Spirit of Christ longs to apply to us all that Christ has provided for us!

The Jewish temple where Jesus' miracle of cleansing took place had three divisions. First of all, there was the outer court, open to all Israel. Beyond that was the inner court or holy place where only the white-robed priests carried on their sacred ministry. Beyond the holy place was the most holy place where stood the ark of the covenant, and above it the cherubim and the shekinah glory.

Herein is a perfect analogy to the temple of the human body. As the temple of the Jews was threefold, so is man tripartite. First of all, there is the *body* (the outer court). Then there is the *soul* (the holy place), which is the seat of consciousness—of thought will, emotion, and imagination. These, like a family of priests, are meant to minister to God in pure-white robes. Beyond the soul, there is the *spirit* (the most holy place), that part of man which is most like God and which is capable of becoming God-filled and God-controlled.

But even though all may become temples of the living God (for all are potential temples), all men are

not such. In many cases, in fact in most cases, the
holiest chamber of the living temple (the spirit) is
empty and given over to darkness and neglect. It is
only at the new birth that the Spirit of Christ enters
and regenerates the spirit of man. Only believers have
the indwelling Spirit, who brings life and salvation.
"He that hath the Son hath the life" (I John 5:12a).
"If any man hath not the Spirit of Christ, he is none
of his" (Rom. 8:9). "He that hath not the Son of God
hath not the life" (I John 5:12b).

In Christ's time, Herod the Great had spent a
tremendous amount of time and money restoring and
beautifying the temple in order to gain the favor of
the Jews. No doubt the priests of that day ministered
exactly according to law; the morning and evening
sacrifices were offered daily; once a year the high
priest entered the holy of holies with blood, performing his proper ministry. But the outer court was
given over to traffic and trade that was neither necessary nor edifying. Pilgrims arriving from foreign
lands needed to purchase animals for sacrifice, and
in order to pay their annual half-shekel, the visitors
also needed to change their money for temple cur-
rency. Yet their needs did not demand that this trade
be carried on in the temple court. Even if trading were
legal, outer-court activities certainly occupied a non-
legal position and received attention out of all proportion to their importance.

Anyone who has visited an Eastern bazaar will understand what confusion, what noise, what defilement,
and what commercialism there must have been in the
outer court of Herod's temple! There, in pens, whole

flocks of sheep and herds of oxen were steaming with heat and filling the sacred edifice with stench and filth.

Today there is a like intrusion of a world-spirit into the Church. Its business is conducted as ordinary business so that there is very little difference between a church meeting and a union meeting, for parliamentary skill is more useful than spirituality. Moreover, the Church has largely adopted the same method of advertising as secular businesses. Fund raising, whether for church or missionary work, is often identical with the March of Dimes or Heart Fund drives. Convert-counting has become a scandal in the church. Extravagant claims of some evangelists sound like the report of an advertising executive. The Church would profit if it considered David's punishment for counting the people of Israel.

In the temple at Jerusalem, everything was in order, according to the letter of the law, but the Spirit was missing; consequently, during Herod's reign, the glory-presence of God was never mentioned. Either it was obscured by merchandise, or long since departed from the holiest place. Hymns of worship and praise were drowned out by price-hagglers. Would-be worshippers had their gold in their hands, trying to strike a sharp bargain for the sacrificial victims.

These conditions of Herod's temple in Jerusalem are a picture of a soul who has chosen the outer court (the body) for his main interest and activity. Moreover, just as Christ cleansed the temple, even so today He wants to cleanse the temple of our bodies. His

scourge of small cords may be small or large circumstances, which he is using to cause us to open the door
to His entrance. But if He is only given permission,
He can drive out everything and anything that does
not belong. We need to know that though sin is weakness, yet Christ is strength. Thus, it matters not how
strong the evil, how deeply or how long it has been
entrenched, if we only open the portal of our life for
His entrance, He will come in, and with love and
power will cleanse our whole being from all impurity.
To be rid of darkness, one needs only to let in the
light; even so, to be delivered from impurity of heart
and life, we must let in the Saviour without bargain-
ing, without haggling, and without bribery. Jesus
Christ must be all or nothing. He will either have all
His way, or He will not enter at all. How He wills
to sanctify wholly! The negative side of sanctification
is cleansing; the positive side is the Baptism with the
Holy Spirit. He wants to do both—to cleanse from
all sin and to baptize with His own wonderful Holy
Spirit.

Which department of our being is ruling—our
body, or our spirit (indwelt by the Holy Spirit)? Are
sheep, oxen, or even gentle doves intruding and oc-
cupying too important a position in our lives? Or is
it the gold of the money-changers which has found
such a place of importance that proper worship is
impossible? Maybe passions, covetousness, fear, worry,
and rush have invaded the outer court and are drawing the attention of our souls from the things of God.
Paul says, "Walk by the Spirit, and ye shall not
fulfil the lust of the flesh." Continually, we must choose

to be influenced by the body or by the Spirit. To choose the body to rule is to become carnal; to choose the Spirit is to be spiritual.

This miracle of the cleansing of the temple was a sign indicating Jesus' authority. "Destroy this temple," said Jesus, "and in three days I *will raise it up*" (that is, "I will resurrect it"). To all hearts who will give Christ permission, His resurrection life will come in with new love, with power, with grace, and with holiness, not only driving out the kingdom of darkness, but also setting up His new kingdom of grace. "I beseech you therefore, brethren, by the mercies of God, to *present your bodies a living sacrifice*, holy, acceptable to God, which is your spiritual service" (Rom 12:1). "Having therefore these promises, beloved, let us cleanse ourselves from all defilement of flesh and spirit, perfecting holiness in the fear of God" (II Cor. 7:1).

CHAPTER TEN

THE BAPTISM WITH THE HOLY SPIRIT

> "Jesus stood and cried, saying, . . . He that believeth on me, as the scripture hath said, from within him shall flow *rivers of living water*. But this spake he of the Spirit, which they that believed on him were to receive: for the Spirit was not yet given; because Jesus was not yet glorified" (John 7:37–39).

IN Christian experience there is nothing more important than the Baptism with the Holy Spirit. Yet concerning this great subject there is less knowledge and more confusion and ignorance than there is concerning almost any other experience in the Christian life. The enemy of our souls first tries his utmost to keep a sinner from experiencing regeneration; then, failing in that, he blinds the newborn soul regarding the truth of sanctification, which includes the Baptism with the Holy Spirit. We are aware that in the broad sense, sanctification includes the whole Christian experience from regeneration to glorification. In a narrower sense, however, the term sanctification is also used in referring to a crisis experience subsequent to regeneration in which one is cleansed from all sin, filled

with perfect love, and also baptized with the Holy
Spirit (who gives the power to live a victorious and
fruitful Christian life).

We take it for granted that all of us understand
that before entering into the more positive side of
sanctification (the Baptism with the Holy Spirit),
there must have been proper preparation made—
that is, an acceptance and embracing of the Cross of
Calvary. This cannot be over-emphasized. Full surrender to God, faith in the blood to cleanse from sins,
and faith in the Cross to cleanse from inner sinfulness are of the utmost importance if one desires to be
a candidate for the Baptism with the Holy Spirit.

That there is much objection to this truth of the
Baptism with the Holy Spirit, we are well aware. For
instance, there is objection to using the term baptism
for this experience. Though several other terms are in
use, we prefer using the term baptism in order to
distinguish it from the indwelling of the Holy Spirit.
Thus the Holy Spirit *indwells* every Christian who has
been genuinely regenerated, enabling him to live a
victorious life; but the Holy Spirit *comes upon* or
baptizes in order to give power and boldness for
effective service. The *life* of a Christian begins at the
Cross; his *service* begins at Pentecost.

There is no question that the Baptism with the
Holy Spirit is also called the filling with the Holy
Spirit. The reason for this is that the disciples at Pentecost were baptized and filled with the Spirit simultaneously. (Today, too, the baptism and the filling happen
at the same time—even as justification and regeneration

do.) Thus the experience may be referred to by either the term baptism or filling, the one always implying the other. However, it *is* right to call the initial experience the Baptism with the Spirit. This in Scripture is followed by *repeated fillings* for special needs. Peter, for instance, was "filled" in Acts 2:4 and also in Acts 4:31.

Concerning the term, the filling of the Spirit, we have often heard the objection, "It isn't that we receive more of the Spirit; it's that He receives more of us." To prove this point, some say, "The Holy Spirit is a Person, and since He is a Person, you receive Him—that is, all of Him. You cannot receive just part of Him since He is a definite Person; it is just a matter of His receiving more of us." Now at first this sounds good, but upon further consideration, we see that it is most illogical. If we cannot receive more or less of the Spirit because He is a Person, how then can the Holy Spirit receive more or less of us, for we are also persons? This argument therefore breaks down and is unworthy of consideration.

If we really want to receive the Baptism with the Holy Spirit, we must also get over another hurdle— namely, the teaching so prevalent today that the Baptism with the Holy Spirit is experienced *simultaneously with* regeneration. As we read the biographies of men who have been mightily used of God, we find that almost without exception they testify to having been filled with the Spirit *subsequent to* regeneration. (Though experiences of course are not the final criterion, five minutes of experience would correct much error in theology!)

There are several direct references to the Baptism with the Holy Spirit in the Scriptures. Each of the Gospels contains John the Baptist's statement regarding this experience. He contrasts it with his own baptism of repentance (Matt. 3:11; Mark 1:8; Luke 3:16; John 1:33). The term is also used by *Jesus Christ* himself in Acts 1:5: "John indeed baptized with water; but ye shall be baptized in [or with] the Holy Spirit not many days hence." *Peter* uses the expression in Acts 11:15-17 where he also describes it as "falling upon" and "the gift." The *Apostle Paul* uses the expression in I Corinthians 12:13: "In one Spirit were we all baptized into one body, whether Jews or Greeks, whether bond or free, and were all made to drink of one Spirit." Many writers and teachers build their whole doctrine of the filling of the Spirit upon this last reference. However, Paul had in mind an entirely different subject, for he was speaking of every believer having been quickened from the dead by the agency of the Holy Spirit and thus made a member of Christ's mystical body. This was the Pauline way of stating the new birth of John 3:7.

Let us now consider this experience of Jesus, of the disciples, and of today's believers. Jesus was *born* of the Spirit and all His life was *indwelt* by the Spirit, but until He was *baptized* with the Holy Spirit, He did not enter into His public ministry. Likewise the disciples. They were believers before Calvary, for Jesus had said they were not of this world and that their names were written in heaven (John 17:16; Luke 10:20); and although on the evening of that Resurrection Day Jesus breathed on them and said, "Receive ye the Holy Spirit" (John 20:20), yet not until fifty days later on the Feast of Pentecost did they experience the Baptism with the Holy Spirit. It was then that they were baptized and filled with the Holy Spirit for service (Acts 2:4).

And so it is today in the normal Christian experience. Every Christian is first born of the Spirit *and* indwelt by the Spirit, for "if any man hath not the Spirit of Christ, he is none of his" (Rom. 8:9). Certainly the more one yields to the Spirit, the more areas there will be for the Spirit to indwell. But, until the Baptism with the Spirit, this indwelling will never be complete. Thus, the indwelling of the Spirit *in* God's servant must not be confused with the Spirit *coming upon* God's servant to give boldness and power for service. It is this latter experience that is rightly called the Baptism with the Holy Spirit or, as some call it, the filling with the Holy Spirit, for He both clothes with power and fills at the same time.

Briefly, we must consider another objection that some raise against this wonderful experience. Some say that because the Holy Spirit was given to the Church at Pentecost, therefore every Christian already has this Pentecostal experience. When we compare this objection with John 3:16 where it says, "God so loved *the world*, that he gave his only begotten Son," then the objection breaks down. For in exactly the same way that Christ is God's gift to the world but everyone has not received Him, so the Holy Spirit is God's gift to the Church, but many in the Church have not received the gift of His Spirit offered them. In both cases there must be a definite personal appropriation.

Again we want to state clearly that we know every Christian *has* the Spirit. But at the same time, we also know that every Christian is not *filled* with the Spirit. To have the Holy Spirit "resident" is a different thing from having him "president"—by which we mean the experience (available for every Christian) of being Spirit-filled, Spirit-controlled, and Spirit-empowered. And is not power the need of the hour? Today this is the universal cry from Christians, especially from those in full-time Christian service. We personally heard their cry, both in the homeland and in more than a score of other countries which we visited. "How can I receive power to serve the Lord effectively?" "I do not have the power I need." "I am so weak and do not have the power that the Bible offers." Everywhere it was made plain that *holiness* and *power* were the crying needs.

One of the familiar passages so frequently referred to concerning the receiving of the Holy Spirit is found in John 7. On the last day, the great day of the Feast of Tabernacles, Jesus had already drawn all eyes toward himself by His superabundant power and teaching. Then He made His great invitation: "If any man thirst, let him come unto me and drink. . . . But this spake he of the Spirit, which they that believed on him were to receive: for the Spirit was *not yet* given; because Jesus was not yet glorified" (John 7:37–39).

This last day of the feast, a Sabbath, was distinguished by very remarkable ceremonies. At a rather solemn moment, the priest brought forth water in golden vessels from the stream of Siloam, which flowed under the temple mountain, and poured it upon the altar. Then the joyousness of the feast broke out in loud jubilation as they sang the Hallel (Psalms 113–118) and Isaiah 12:3: "With joy shall ye draw water out of the wells of salvation." This ceremony was commemorative of Moses' smiting the rock in Horeb, followed by the flowing of the historic stream of water, for "the Lord said unto Moses, . . . Take . . . thy rod, wherewith thou smotest the river, . . . and thou shalt smite the rock, and *there shall come water out of it*, that the people may drink" (Ex. 17:5, 6, A.V.). It was at this precise moment when all were thinking of the rock and the stream of water flowing from it that Jesus gave that great invitation, "If any man thirst, let him come unto me and drink."

That rock in Horeb was a type of Christ, for Paul said, "They drank of a spiritual rock that followed them, and the rock was Christ" (I Cor. 10:4). Thus the smitten rock in Horeb, from which the water gushed out, set forth the death of Jesus on the Cross under the stroke of divine judgment. But the water that flowed out was a type of the Holy Spirit, for the Bible never refers to water as a type of Christ, but rather refers to Christ as the giver of the water of the Holy Spirit. Thus, the flowing of the waters from the rock foreshadowed the outpouring of the living water of the Holy Spirit (which proceeded from Christ when He, the Rock, was smitten on Calvary). The water suggests the cleansing, refreshing, satisfying influences of the blessed Comforter. In John 7:38 Jesus said, "He that believeth on me, . . . from within him shall flow rivers of living water"; then Jesus went on to say, "for the Spirit was not yet given." Why was He not yet given? Because at the time at which Jesus was speaking,

Calvary had not yet come. Calvary in Scripture is closely associated with Pentecost, and the precious blood of the Lord Jesus with the Comforter. We cannot have the Holy Spirit apart from the Cross of Jesus Christ.

All this is clearly seen in the Old Testament in the consecration of the priests, for the *oil* was always poured upon the *blood* (Lev. 8:24, 30). Likewise, in the cleansing of the leper, first the blood of the trespass offering, then the oil, was placed on the right ear, the right thumb, and the right great toe (Lev. 14: 25, 28). In his epistle, John connects Calvary and Pentecost in the piercing of Jesus' side by the Roman soldier, for he says, "This is he that came by water and blood, even Jesus Christ; not with the water only, but with the water and with the blood. And it is the Spirit that beareth witness, because the Spirit is the truth" (I John 5:6, 7). Therefore in pursuance of Christ's finished work, the Holy Spirit was poured out at Pentecost. In a real sense, Pentecost is never repeated any more than Calvary, but as the benefits of Calvary must be received, so must the benefits of Pentecost be received.

But how is the Baptism with the Holy Spirit received? God's Word says, "Received ye the Spirit by the works of the law, or *by the hearing of faith?*" (Gal. 3:2); and again, "He therefore that supplieth to you the Spirit, and worketh miracles among you, doeth he it by the works of the law, or *by the hearing of faith?*" (Gal. 3:5); "[Ye] receive the promise of the Spirit *through faith*" (Gal. 3:14). The way of receiving this blessing is not by works, nor by law, nor by excitement or noisy demonstration. The only way to receive the Baptism with the Spirit is *by faith*.

But why have so few received this gift? Because this gift is for the thirsty, and so few are thirsty. If one is living in sin, there is no thirst. Drinking of the world's cisterns never really satisfies and will take away the keen edge of the real thirst (that causes one to come to Christ for this great gift).

Another important fact that we need to understand is that it is Jesus Christ who gives this gift. From His own invitation in John 7 and also from the words of John the Baptist, we learn that Jesus Christ is the Baptizer. John the Baptist said to the multitudes, "I indeed baptize you in water unto repentance: but *he* that cometh after me . . . *shall baptize you* in the Holy Spirit and in fire" (Matt. 3:11). Jesus himself stated that *He* is the One that gives the Holy Spirit: "If I go not away, the Comforter will not come unto you; but if I go, *I will send* him unto you" (John 16:7). Peter also definitely designated Jesus Christ as the One who poured out the Spirit in that wonderful experience, for he said on the day of Pentecost, "Being therefore by the right hand of God exalted, and having received of the Father the promise of the Holy Spirit, *he hath poured forth this*, which ye see and hear" (Acts 2:33). This verse clearly shows that after His exaltation, it was Jesus Christ himself who received this wonderful gift and who now pours it forth (gives it). Thus, from first to last, Jesus Christ remains the center of our Christian experience. This is very important and absolutely essential, lest one be led off from the truth of the centrality of Jesus Christ.

"If any man *thirst*, let him come unto me and *drink*," Jesus said. Thus Jesus compared this experience of receiving the Baptism with the Holy Spirit to a thirsty man drinking water. And how does one drink? Drinking is the easiest and most natural thing in the world for a person to do. One who is thirsty does not have to be taught *how* to drink, for he simply opens his mouth and takes in. Drinking is as easy as that. The application is clear. The Holy Spirit is a definite Person and though we cannot see Him, He is all around us. Like the air, He is here and at the same time in China and in Africa and in India. In receiving the Baptism with the Spirit, it may help to tell the Lord, "I know that the Spirit is here. I am thirsty for Him; I want Him. May He come upon me now. May He fill me now. Just as I breathe in this air, I receive Thy wonderful Holy Spirit."

F. B. Meyer's experience of the Baptism with the Holy Spirit may prove both interesting and helpful to those who are seeking the Lord. In his book *The Christ-Life for the Self-Life* he writes:

> I had been a minister of a large influential church, but I was very unhappy, for I was conscious that I had not received the power of the Holy Ghost. Then I went up to that little village, Keswick, where a great number of God's people had gathered to seek and receive the power of the Holy Spirit. One night they had elected to have a prayer meeting from nine o'clock to eleven and onwards to pray for the Holy Ghost. I joined them and found a great many people were agonizing. But I was too tired to agonize, and somehow felt that God did not want me to agonize hour after hour. *I had to learn to take.* God wanted to give! I had

only to take. That is what little children do at
meal time. For instance, tomorrow your little
girl will come down to breakfast very hungry.
The bread and milk, or the oatmeal is on the
table. You do not say, "Little girlie, run up-
stairs and agonize, roll on the floor for an
hour, and then come down." You say, "Little
one, I am so glad you have a good appetite.
Now there is your chair; in you get; say your
prayer; and start away." That is what God
says to the soul. All nights of prayer for the
Holy Ghost are principally necessary to get
people who pray into a fit condition to receive
the Holy Ghost; for when the people are ready,
the Holy Ghost will come without agonizing.

So, I left that prayer meeting at Keswick.
It was eleven o'clock or half past ten, and I
crept out into the lane away from the village.
As I walked I said, "Oh my God, if there is
a man in this village who needs the power of
the Holy Ghost to rest upon him, it is I; but
I do not know how to receive Him. I am too
tired, too worn, too nervously down to agonize."

A voice said to me, "As you took forgiveness from the hand of the dying Christ, *take
the Holy Ghost* from the hand of the living
Christ."

I turned to Christ and said, "Lord, as I
breathe in this whiff of warm night air, so I
breathe into every part of me Thy blessed
Spirit." I felt no hand laid upon my head;
there was no lambent flame; there was no
rushing sound from heaven. *But by faith*, without emotion and without excitement, I took for
the first time, *and I have kept on taking ever
since.*

I turned to leave the mountain side, and
as I went down, the tempter said, "You have
got nothing. It is moonshine."

I said, "I have."
He said, "Do you feel it?"
I said, "I do not."
"Then if you do not feel it, you have not got it."
I said, "I do not feel it, but I reckon that God is faithful, and He could not have brought a hungry soul to claim the Holy Spirit by faith, and then have given a stone for bread, and a scorpion for fish. I know I have Him because God led me to put in my claim."

May every thirsty soul come to Jesus and ask Him for the Baptism and the filling with the Holy Spirit. Need we repeat that this blessing is only for those who have fully surrendered to God and who have been cleansed from all sin? Do what F. B. Meyer and many others have done. Make application to Jesus. Tell Him you know He is the One to whom the gift is given; speak to the Rock; by faith ask and receive from Him the gift of the Holy Spirit. God will give assurance that this gift is now yours.

If one truly receives the Spirit by faith, he will receive the witness of the Spirit that it is so, for one knows when he has been baptized with the Spirit, and there is evidence of the Baptism with the Holy Spirit. For instance, if I am blind, I ask my friend concerning the landscape:
"Are there mountains?"
He answers, "Yes."
"Rivers?"
"Yes."
"Cornfields?"
"Yes."

In my blindness I ask question after question and get what help I can. But when my eyes are opened or when the light of the morning breaks, *because I see it for myself*, I ask no more questions about the contour and the configuration of the landscape.

One infallible evidence is found in John 16:13, 14: "When he, the Spirit of truth, is come . . . he shall glorify me." The flesh cannot glorify Christ, nor can the devil. Only the indwelling Holy Ghost can truly glorify Him. When He has come upon us and filled us, He will glorify the Son.

Another evidence of this experience is the fruit of the Spirit: "love, joy, peace, longsuffering, kindness, goodness, faithfulness, meekness, self-control" (Gal. 5: 22, 23). Now these are not nine fruits—but the description of one—love. These additional eight words give us quality, quantity, and flavors of the first fruit —love. If we have love, we have the other eight; if we lack love, we lack all.

Let me also say that one who has received the gift will have that inner knowledge which precludes the necessity for any further evidence that he is both *baptized and filled with the Holy Ghost* just as there is an inner knowing that one is *born* of God, *washed* in His blood, *delivered* from the power of Satan and the self-life.

One more evidence of having been baptized with the Spirit is this: one with such an experience is also equipped and endowed with those gifts of the Spirit enumerated in I Corinthians 12, 13 and 14. For in-

stance, soon such a one finds a desire to praise the
Lord with his whole heart—not only with all the
words he knows, but with words that only the Holy
Spirit can give. Thus, for the glory of Jesus and the
fulfillment of His commission for soul-winning and the
evangelization of the world, the Holy Spirit will give
these gifts for power and for revelation and for utterance. Praise be to the Father, Son, and Holy Spirit.
Amen.

CHAPTER ELEVEN

"CLOTHED WITH POWER FROM ON HIGH"

"Elijah said. . . , Ask what I shall do
for thee, before I am taken from thee.
And Elisha said, I pray thee, let a
double portion of thy spirit be upon
me" (II Kings 2:9).

I F there is an audible cry in the Church today,
especially among pastors and workers, it is the cry
for power. Some have given up this quest; others are
continuing their search, though quite often they are
either too prejudiced or too lacking in knowledge of
the ways of God to receive it. No matter whether darkness be from teaching or lack of teaching, for any true
seeker, Elisha's experience with Elijah will give light,
instruction, inspiration, and challenge on this most
important subject of being "clothed with power from
on high" (Luke 24:49).

"Elijah took his mantle, and wrapped it together, and smote the waters, and they were
divided hither and thither, so that they two
went over on dry ground. And it came to
pass, as they still went on, and talked. that,
. . . Elijah went up by a whirlwind into heaven.
. . . He [Elisha] took up also the mantle of

143

Elijah that fell from him, and went back, and stood by the bank of the Jordan. And he... smote the waters, and said, Where is Jehovah, the God of Elijah? and when he also had smitten the waters, they were divided hither and thither; and Elisha went over" (II Kings 2:8, 11, 13, 14).

In I Kings 19:15–21 we read that Elijah, the mighty miracle-working prophet, was told by God to anoint his successor to be prophet in his stead. And so, he came upon Elisha plowing in the fields of his father's farm. Thereupon, Elijah "cast his mantle upon him" (the symbol of the prophet's office and power). Touched by that mantle, Elisha burned his bridges behind him, said goodbye to his parents, and followed the prophet. This mantle-touch, or rather that which the mantle-touch symbolized, made Elisha a changed man. From that moment on, he was *a committed soul.*

How long Elisha was a disciple of Elijah, we do not know, for we are only told that he "ministered unto Elijah." His ministry for this period was doubtless a succession of menial tasks of a servant. What a pattern for Christian ministers today!

But Elisha is also our example of a "going-on Christian." Though touched by the prophet's mantle, and though committed wholly to the service of God, Elisha was not satisfied. There had awakened in him a desire for *all* that the prophet's mantle symbolized. And so when the time came for Elijah's translation, Elisha "went with him"—first to Gilgal, then to Bethel, and finally to Jericho. These three places were rich in memory—doubtless suggesting to Elisha (as the meanings and associations connected with these names may also suggest to us) thoughts of communion, of vision, of relationship, and of victory. In each of these places Elisha was told he could stay; in fact, Elijah tested him by urging him to stay. But until Elisha was clothed by the mantle, he refused to be stopped by any thing, or any one (even Elijah), or to remain at any place.

Finally "they two stood by the Jordan." There Elijah did not tell Elisha to tarry, as he had counselled at the other places—for Jordan stands for Calvary. When one gets there, he must cross at once. There is no need to send spies to spy out the land on the other side. Far more often than not, spies bring evil reports. Is it not true today, too, that whenever anyone considers this crisis of full consecration to God and of all that identification with Christ crucified may mean, including the Baptism with the Holy Spirit, the devil has a whole company of professional spies ready to volunteer their services? While standing too long by the Jordan, many are frightened away. Therefore, on this occasion Elijah did *not* tarry at the Jordan but took his mantle (the symbol of power) and smote the waters with it. "When they were divided hither and thither," Elijah and Elisha went over on dry land. Even so, we today are not to be satisfied just to be near the Cross. We are to "cross over" by dying to self and the world (with all of its implications and associations). We must be "clean over Jordan."

Elisha's preparations were now completed, so Elijah said to Elisha, "Ask what I shall do for thee, before I am taken from thee."

Quickly and clearly the answer came, "Let a double portion of thy spirit be upon me."

"Thou hast asked a *hard* thing," said Elijah.

Let us stop to consider this phrase further. This thing which Elisha wanted—anointing with power from on high—was to be received from God by faith as a gift. But it is called a *hard* thing—hard for the natural man. In order for the reign and dynamic of the Holy Spirit to be established, the old *natural* powers must be deposed—whether originating in man's spirit or in his soul or in his body. Even for the prepared soul, this will not be easy but will require definite concentration, for Elisha was told, "*If thou see me* when I am taken from thee, it shall be so unto thee; but *if not*, it shall not be so." From the first, Elisha had been a committed soul. Now, however, he had to be a *concentrating soul*. This is where many break down. It is comparatively easy to get people interested for a while in the fullness of the power of Pentecost, but it is difficult to maintain desire and interest until the time comes when one is actually clothed with power from on high. Therefore "it is a *hard* thing."

Elisha, however, kept his eyes on Elijah and *saw* the prophet taken up to heaven! Then, taking hold of his own garment (the symbol of his own natural power) and tearing it in two pieces, he took up Elijah's mantle which had fallen to the earth. This was the same mantle that years before had changed Elisha's life and given him a desire to be "clothed upon" with power from on high. *Now* that desire was satisfied, for Elisha had the mantle—*he had the power* that the mantle symbolized.

Immediately, Elisha reckoned on the new power now his. Going back to the Jordan, he struck the waters with the mantle. Straightway they parted, and he went over on dry land. In full assurance of faith in his new experience with the power from on high, Elisha now continued to trust God to manifest that miraculous power through him. He was not disappointed. And so, though seven miracles of Elijah are recorded for us in the Word, twice as many are recorded of Elisha. (For example, Elijah raised *one* from the dead, but Elisha two.) May these facts, revealed for us in the Scriptures, help us believe that Elisha actually received what he requested—a double portion of the spirit of Elijah. (This "double portion" may also refer to the inheritance of the firstborn.)

Today, all Christians should be clothed with power from on high. All are *touched* by the Spirit (as Elisha was touched by the mantle of Elijah when Elijah cast it over him), but all are not *clothed* with the power of the Spirit. Even though born of the Spirit, changed by His touch and His indwelling, and possessing the "earnest" of this wonderful blessing, no Christian should be satisfied without the fullness of the Spirit. Yielding more and more to the indwelling Spirit means we are more and more filled with the Spirit. But yet this is *not* being clothed with power from on high. The Holy Spirit *within* enriches the inner life; the Holy Spirit *upon* anoints with power for service.

In conclusion, it is well to be warned by one more detail from the story of Elisha. On the day of Elisha's anointing, the sons of the prophets, fifty of them, were near to Elijah and Elisha. Twice they saw the miraculous parting of the Jordan. They also knew that Jehovah had "taken away" Elijah. Yet though so near and having witnessed so much, *not one* of these fifty sons of the prophets were clothed with power. So today, it is possible to know about power from on high, to talk about it, and to be near it, but not to experience it. Lest we be like the fifty sons of the prophets—just onlookers—may we each commit ourselves wholly to God and His purposes, and without distraction concentrate on receiving God's wonderful gift of power from on high.

CHAPTER TWELVE

TOO MUCH EMPHASIS ON THE HOLY SPIRIT?

> "I will pray the Father, and he shall
> give you another Comforter, that he
> may be with you for ever, even the
> Spirit of truth: . . . ye know him; for
> he abideth with you, and shall be in
> you" (John 14:16, 17).

NOT long ago someone said of us: "Too much emphasis is given to the Holy Spirit. Everyone will be seeking the Baptism with the Holy Spirit if they keep this up. Besides that, they shouldn't use the term *the Baptism with the Holy Spirit*."

Yes, many today cringe at the words, the Baptism with the Holy Spirit. They rather prefer the term *filling*, since that does not imply a definite crisis and can therefore be more gradual. Others believe that the term, the Baptism with the Spirit, has a sectarian connotation. But if it does, then John the Baptist was sectarian, and so also was Jesus Christ, and the Apostle Peter! Besides, though Luther rediscovered the truth of justification by faith, and every born-again Christian believes in it—that does not make him a Lutheran. Likewise, Wesley rediscovered the truth of sanctification by faith, and many have the witness of the

Spirit to this wonderful experience—but that does not make them Methodists. William Booth gave himself to the down-and-outers—but those who have a real burden for reclaiming derelicts and who give themselves to that ministry are not necessarily Salvation Army people. Several Pentecostal denominations are flourishing today, and some of them no doubt were used by God to rediscover for the Church that wonderful experience which is rightly called the Baptism with the Holy Spirit. But the term, the Baptism with the Holy Spirit, is no more sectarian than justification by faith, or sanctification by faith, or rescue mission work.

John the Baptist was neither ashamed nor afraid of the term, the Baptism with the Holy Spirit. Nor was Jesus Christ, nor the Apostle Peter, nor Charles G. Finney, nor A. B. Simpson, nor R. A. Torrey, nor A. J. Gordon, nor Andrew Murray, nor Jonathan Goforth, nor Dwight L. Moody. Neither should we be afraid either of the term or the definite experience. There is no more denominational monopoly on this blessing than on justification and sanctification, for it is *for every Christian* in the Church universal.

The Baptism with the Holy Spirit is an experience plainly set forth in the Word of God, and anyone entering into it should not find it necessary to leave one evangelical church in order to become a member of another evangelical church that considers this experience the central plank of its platform. But many are forced to leave and go elsewhere because of resistance to and refusal of this doctrine of the Baptism with the Spirit. Yet, as we have said, God would have *every member* of His body not only justified and sanctified, but also *baptized and filled with the Holy Spirit*— so that each might live a holy life and have a passionate interest in God's great missionary program at home and abroad. Of course it is true that to be forgiven one's sins and to be born of God is the most wonderful thing that can happen to the sinner. But to the Christian, being sanctified and baptized with the Holy Spirit is the most wonderful blessing that he can receive.

Many would prefer to call this experience by the term *filled* with the Spirit. (Other terms used in the Bible are the gift of the Holy Spirit, the promise of the Father, and clothed with power from on high.) Nevertheless, we have discovered that he who objects to the term the *Baptism* with the Spirit has a very difficult time getting *filled* with the Spirit, for there usually is a reason for the objection.

The same thing is true regarding the gifts of the Spirit mentioned in I Corinthians 12. Anyone who disparages a single one of the Spirit's gifts will find difficulty in receiving *any* of them; in fact, he is generally void both of the grace of the Holy Spirit and of His power. We do *not* believe that any of the gifts of the Spirit are given as special evidence that one is baptized with the Spirit, but one who has this wonderful experience is qualified to exercise the gifts of the Spirit as given in I Corinthians 12. A man is not baptized with the Spirit *because* he exercises the gifts of the Spirit; on the contrary, he exercises the gifts *because* he is baptized with the Spirit. Actually the Spirit's gifts are *manifestations of the Holy Spirit* in different ministries as the Spirit wills, and so none of these gifts should be disparaged or called of small account. Since they are gifts of love from God, it is not proper to call any of them unimportant or little, even though we may call some of them greater gifts.

Though we are presenting in the simplest of terms the truth of the Baptism with the Holy Spirit (and its accompanying blessings and resultant gifts and powers), we want it clearly understood that the message of the Cross is still our central teaching. Before we can be considered a candidate for the Baptism with the Holy Spirit, we must clearly see Christ dying as man's Substitute and as man's Representative. We must never emphasize the Person and the Work of the Holy Spirit at the expense of the Person and Work of Christ, the Son of God, our Redeemer. But yet we need not be afraid of the Holy Spirit, for He will lead us to Calvary first, and then to Pentecost.

Now we need not expect that there will be another historic Pentecost any more than there will be another historic Calvary. Christ is *God's* gift to the world; the Holy Spirit is *Christ's* gift to the Church. Thus, just as a *sinner* in the act of salvation needs to become rightly related to the truth of Calvary, so *Christians* should become rightly related to the central truth of Pentecost. And just as each sinner in the world must *personally* receive the gift of Christ as Saviour, so each Christian in the Church must *personally* receive the gift of the Holy Spirit. Jesus promised that He would pray the Father to give *"another Comforter, that he may be with you for ever, even the Spirit of truth: whom the world cannot receive; for it beholdeth him not, neither knoweth him: ye know*

him; for he abideth *with* you, and shall be *in* you"
(John 14:16, 17).

Many have robbed themselves of this wonderful
experience of the Baptism with the Holy Spirit by
accepting non-scriptural, dispensational teaching. That
the present dispensation is different from that of the
Old Testament we all accept; for if it were not, we
would be carrying a lamb to church instead of a hymn
book. But there are other intricate, man-made divisions
of dispensations, which tend to minister to pride (rather
than to humility and faith) and thus rob us of blessing.
Though the Holy Spirit carefully guards the truth of
Calvary and Pentecost, yet many have missed great
blessing by relegating God's distinctive revelations to a
dispensational and transitional period. Christians "write
off" experience and examples given to us in God's Word
as a product of the time of transition! "Experiences do
not apply," they say; "it is different now." Yes, I
should say it is different—far too different, for *then*
the apostles and their followers had great power,
whereas *today* the Church is experiencing little or no
power. It is much easier to explain the truth away than
be willing either to seek the promise of the Father or
meet the conditions for receiving Him. But oh, what
loss!

The writer can give personal testimony to the experience of the Baptism with the Holy Spirit. He was
born of God, had the Spirit's witness of supernatural
regeneration, and for many years was living in fellowship with the indwelling Christ by the Spirit. Yet a
time came when he was baptized with the Holy Spirit

in a definite crisis experience. This gave him an entirely new conception of Christ and His nearness, a new desire to pray and worship, and a new power for service. Even the Bible became a new book. Oh that Christians everywhere would seek for and be baptized with the Holy Spirit! At Pentecost the disciples were baptized and filled with the Spirit; and since Pentecost every believer may be baptized with the Holy Spirit and receive this wonderful Gift from Christ—a Gift given Him by the Father for the Church.

There are those who say that any emphasis on the Holy Spirit (especially the Baptism with the Holy Spirit) brings division. The answer to this fear is that division comes only when and where there is resistance to the truth; then, of course, there is division, as truth always divides asunder when met by resistance (whether on the doctrines of salvation and sanctification, or the Baptism with the Spirit).

Many today have lived so long at such a slow dying rate that when this *normal Christian experience* manifests itself in certain believers, it is not recognized as a work of the Spirit of God. What a terrible loss and tragedy to any church such a situation must be! How it must "grieve" and "quench" and "do despite to" the Spirit of grace! On the other hand, if God's Word in chapters 14, 15, and 16 of John's Gospel (and other related passages) is really studied, one will soon be persuaded to seek and receive God's wonderful blessing—the Baptism with the Holy Spirit. To this end, study out the following references to the Holy Spirit.

In the Gospels

"I indeed baptize you in water unto repentance: but he that cometh after me is mightier than I, whose shoes I am not worthy to bear: he shall *baptize you in the Holy Spirit and in fire*" (Matt. 3:11).

"Behold, I send forth the promise of the Father upon you: but tarry ye in the city, until ye *be clothed with power from on high*" (Luke 24:49).

"I will pray the Father, and he shall give you *another Comforter*, that he may be with you for ever, even the Spirit of truth: whom the world cannot receive; for it beholdeth him not, neither knoweth him: ye shall know him; for he abideth with you, and shall be in you. I will not leave you desolate: I come unto you" (John 14:16–18).

"These things have I spoken unto you, while yet abiding with you. But *the Comforter*, even the Holy Spirit, whom the Father will send in my name, he shall teach you all things, and bring to your remembrance all that I have said unto you" (John 14:25, 26).

"When *the Comforter* is come, whom I will send unto you from the Father, even *the Spirit of truth*, which proceedeth from the Father, he shall bear witness of me" (John 15:26).

"Nevertheless I tell you the truth: It is expedient for you that I go away; for if I go not away, *the Comforter* will not come unto you; but if I go, I will send him unto you. And he, when he is come, will convict the world in respect of sin, and of righteousness, and of judgment: of sin, because they believe not on me; of righteousness, because I go to the Father, and ye behold me no more; of judgment, because the prince of this world hath been judged. I have yet many things to say unto you, but ye cannot bear them now. Howbeit when he, *the Spirit of truth*, is come, he shall guide you into all the truth: for he shall not speak from himself; but what things soever he shall hear, these shall he speak: and he shall declare unto you the things that are to come. He shall glorify me: for he shall take of mine, and shall declare it unto you. All things whatsoever the Father hath are mine: therefore said I, that he taketh of mine, and shall declare it unto you" (John 16:7–15).

In the Acts of the Apostles

"John indeed baptized with water; but ye shall be *baptized in [with] the Holy Spirit* not many days hence" (1:5).

"Ye shall receive *power, when the Holy Spirit is come upon you:* and ye shall be my witnesses both in Jerusalem, and in all Judea and Samaria, and unto the uttermost part of the earth" (1:8).

"When the day of Pentecost was now come, they were all together in one place. And suddenly there came from heaven *a sound* as of the rushing of a mighty wind, and it filled all the house where they were sitting. And there appeared unto them tongues parting asunder, like as of fire; and it sat upon each one of them. And they were all *filled with the Holy Spirit*, and began to speak with other tongues, as the Spirit gave them utterance" (2:1–4).

"Being therefore by the right hand of God exalted, and having received of the Father *the promise of the Holy Spirit*, he hath poured forth this, which ye see and hear" (2:33).

CHAPTER THIRTEEN

THE DAILY APPLICATION OF THE CROSS— DISCIPLINE

"The fruit of the Spirit is. . . self-control"
(Gal. 5:22, 23).

BEFORE we begin a detailed study of the third aspect of the Cross, *Christ Crucified IN Us*, it may be helpful to review very briefly the first two aspects of the Cross discussed in chapters 1–4. First of all, we considered the aspect, *Christ Crucified FOR Us*, which deals with unregenerate man and makes possible the forgiveness of sins and assurance of eternal life. This crisis experience of the new birth takes place when any man or woman, boy or girl fulfills the God-given conditions of repentance and faith.

Then we considered the second crossroad, sanctification, an experience as conscious and as definite as salvation. We learned that Christ was crucified *as* us, even as the Apostle Paul wrote to the Corinthians: "One died for all, therefore all died; and he [Christ] died for all, that they that live should *no longer* live *unto themselves*, but *unto him*" (II Cor. 5:14, 15). Again one must make a choice—this time *choosing to die* (to sin, to self, to the world, and to the devil), to surrender fully to Christ, and to become truly "alive unto God."

Before we go on to study the discipline of the believer's body by the Holy Spirit, it is absolutely essential to re-emphasize the crisis of sanctification. If the great blessing of sanctification has not been experienced, any discipline would be merely trying to improve the old man, and this would be impossible. The Scriptures declare that the old man *is* dead, for Christ embraced the whole sinful race and bore us all to Calvary. But it is up to us to consent to this truth (that in union with Christ we have died), and to trust the Holy Spirit to make it so real in our experience that we can go on and do what the Scriptures enjoin us to do—"Reckon [ourselves] . . . dead unto sin, but alive unto God" (Rom. 6:11). Nothing is removed in the crisis of sanctification except sin, for God does not dehumanize us. The old nature is the human nature tainted by sin; the new nature is the human nature purged from sin—the very same nature in a different relationship. As we see it, sanctification is not the eradication of a nature at all but the cleansing of the whole personality of sin. No part of us can or should be removed.

The best illustration of a change of relationships is in the record of the once wild, untamed demoniac who lived in the tombs (Mark 5). No man could tame "him that was possessed of demons." They could not tie him up; he would break the chains. They could not clothe him; he would tear off the clothes. They could not do a thing with him and so were afraid of him.

One day Jesus came and delivered the demoniac from the evil spirits that possessed him. Afterwards, we find this same man sitting at the feet of Jesus, clothed, and in his right mind. He is the same person before and after deliverance. When he was related to the devil, he was wild, tameless, uncontrollable, and dangerous; but when delivered from his relationship with the devil and rightfully related to Christ, he was quiet, loving, harmless, and filled with a strong desire to follow his Deliverer. Why the difference? Because of a change in relationship. Even so is it today. By the Cross, Christ sets the Christian free, delivering him from the power of sin and of the devil.

Even though there is much resistance to the truth of sanctification, we must not by-pass this crisis. The Church today needs the message of sanctification. For lack of proper instruction on this subject, converted people have not gone on with God; therefore we *must* make known this truth. In no other way is the sinfulness of the heart so completely exposed as in its opposition to holiness. Someone once said, "It isn't the doctrine I object to so much, but your constant insistence upon it. You preach it all the time."

The answer was, "That's true, but if *you* preached to defeated, unfruitful Christians, what would you preach?"

The reluctant reply was, "The same thing that you are preaching."

Someone once told a Keswick minister that his preaching was lopsided. "Yes," he remarked, "but I preach to a lopsided people."

There is then a crisis of regeneration, followed by a crisis of sanctification. But after sanctification, then what? What kind of daily life will now be consistent with this profession of freedom from the power of sin and the devil? How shall we live the sanctified life? Having seen that the "old man" needs the Cross (a real denying of self in a conclusive act), we must now go on to see that the "new man" also needs the Cross. This introduces us to the third and still deeper aspect of Christ's Cross—the daily application of the Cross to the new man in daily disciplines, daily sacrifices, daily brokenness, daily intercession, and daily warfare. In Luke 9:23 Jesus goes on from the phrase, "Deny [yourself]," and adds, *"take up [your] cross daily,* and follow me." It is that word *daily* that He emphasizes. The new man that walks in newness of life must be disciplined. Unless the new man bears *a daily cross,* he will have the same old trouble.

Because most of our temptations are addressed to the body, its control is absolutely necessary. Since the devil cannot directly touch the soul's inner relationship to God, he spends most of his time attacking the outer man, the house in which we live. Therefore this outer man must be kept under control and bear a daily cross. The Apostle Paul, speaking of the control of the body, says,

> "And this I do for the gospel's sake, that I might be partaker thereof with you. Know ye not that they which run in a race run all, but one receiveth the prize? So run, that ye may obtain. And every man that striveth for the mastery is temperate in all things. Now they do it to obtain a corruptible crown; but we an

incorruptible. I therefore so run, not as uncertainly; so fight I, not as one that beateth the air: but I keep under my body, and bring it into subjection: lest that by any means, when I have preached to others, I myself should be a castaway" (I Cor. 9:23–27, A.V.).

The real need in the human life is not only that we be cleansed from all sin but also that we get things back into God's order—making the body to be the servant rather than the master. So many have confessed that their prayer life is not what it ought to be and are trying to do something about it. Their only time for real prayer is in the mornings, for their days are so full. But though rising early for several days in succession is comparatively easy, yet soon all kinds of reasonings advise staying in bed a few minutes longer—such as, "It was late last night"; or "I was extra tired"; or "I did not sleep too well." So, because the body has been allowed to dictate, the eyes close again; prayer is forgotten. The body must not have that position. One version translates "buffet my body" "beat black and blue." I must keep my body in control, the spirit ruling, the body obeying and not ruling.

Mathilde Wrede, the cultured daughter of a provincial governor in Finland, well educated and a gifted musician, gave herself over to the Lord in her teens to work out His purposes in her. God called her to minister to criminals in prison. She lived on the same fare as they, and the prisoners loved her for it. Early in the morning she would bring them food and encouragement and then tell them about the Lord, His gift of salvation, and the life in Christ that they could live. All was not easy for her, but she knew by the Spirit how to buffet her body. She spent herself to the utmost. After a sleepless night when she felt almost unable to resume her usual duties, Mathilde would reassure her poor, tired body that it had always cooperated with her in doing her Father's will before, and she was sure it would be patient, loving, and obedient that day also. For Christ's sake and by the power of His Spirit, Mathilde Wrede had her body under control.

Similarly, as a soldier on a battlefield was going "over the top," he once was heard to remark, "Body of mine, if you knew where I'm taking you today, you'd shake more than you're shaking now." That is what it means to bear the daily cross in the matter of discipline. That is the spirit we must have.

Of course, to try to discipline the body by self-energy always fails, for self-control is not of ourselves but is a fruit of the Spirit (Gal. 5:23). True self-control is never separate from the Cross. There is a fleshly attempt to discipline, and there is a spiritual way. The spiritual way is the way of the Cross—yielding gladly on any and every point, in obedience to the Holy Spirit.

To bear the cross daily. costs. Are you doing all things for the gospel's sake? Or do you say: "Others expect too much of me. If it were not that my body says, I'm too tired, I would be witnessing to more souls"? May God save us from pampering or coddling our bodies. Rather, let them be yielded as willing servants. It was said of Jesus that He "was not yet fifty years old." He was only about thirty, but may He not have looked nearer fifty because He had burned himself out in prayer? "In the morning, a great while before day, he rose up and went out, and departed into a desert place, and there prayed" (Mark 1:35). In the original, this passage indicates that it was not an occasional but a continual thing. It was evidently His habit to rob His body of sleep (if necessary) in order to find time for prayer.

Scripture says we are tripartite beings: "May your spirit and soul and body be preserved entire" (I Thess. 5:23). Yet more often than not, this phrase is quoted in the reversed order—body, soul and spirit. Why? Because to us the body is more important than anything else. If you don't believe that for you the body is the most important, just ask yourself, "If I get up too late in the morning for prayers and breakfast, do I skip prayers or do I skip breakfast?" Most of us would skip prayers. How we need this daily cross—not a crisis but a process! The Lord asks us to be a living sacrifice, to be disciplined continually. We are complex beings, but why do we seem more complicated than we really are? Because we are not unified. Because we are out of God's order. The Spirit is *not* directing the life—with the soul interpreting, and the body carrying out the decisions which the spirit dictates.

Through the *spirit* (with its faculties of conscience, worship and intuition) we are God-conscious. Through the *soul* (with its faculties of intellect, emotions, and volition) we are self-conscious. Through the *body* (man's visible part, together with his senses) we are world-conscious. We can not see the real person; we can see only the house in which he lives. But the body is not the important thing. Far more important is the hidden man of the heart—the personality. Therefore we must *not* let the body rule us, but *we* must rule and discipline the body. At the Fall, man was not only tainted by sin but turned wrong side up. Instead of the spirit being supreme, the body became supreme. Though we may not like to agree with this, on checking into many of our decisions, we will find that the spirit actually received very little consideration—at least it received much less than the body. We need to be turned right side up to have the order that God intended.

The running of a factory affords a good illustration: There is an inner office for the proprietor or general manager; there is an outer office, where the clerks and secretaries do their work; and there is the factory, the shop itself. Directions should always come from the *inner* office, then be interpreted and put into force in the *outer* office, and finally be fully executed in the *factory* or the shop. As long as the inner office has control of the outer office and of the factory, everything goes right. But if the outer office workers or the shop workers go on a strike, what happens? There is no production. Unless some solution is found, the business fails, everything is disrupted, and the owner gets no profit out of his investment.

So it is with us. Unless the whole personality is in the God-appointed control, neither God nor our own personal spirit will receive any eternal benefit. Too often the body dictates and demands that this or that appetite or passion should be satisfied. For instance, we are called to minister. But invariably it is at the wrong time—either it is mealtime, or bedtime, or a time when we are all worn out. Usually there is opportunity to refuse. Yet in such cases our feelings should not rule, but rather our own personal spirit indwelt by God. Orders must not come from the body but from God, and God will never call without supplying strength to obey. The body generally tries to bluff us and save itself, but just here we must demonstrate the spirit ruling the body.

The disciplined lives of the Spartans (500 B.C.) are a challenge. The one purpose of their education was to make soldiers. Their young boys were taken from their homes at the age of seven and never slept under their mothers' roofs again. From then on they wore the same weight clothing summer and winter, cooked their own food, and slept on a mat of rushes instead of an ordinary bed. On festival days they were publicly whipped before the altars of their temples to test their endurance. Rather than cry out under the lash, some would die. Spartan training produced strength of body—though hardness of heart. Everybody was trained to live not for himself but for the state.

As a result of disciplining their bodies, Greek military exploits were almost unbelievable. For instance, though outnumbered more than two to one in the Battle of Marathon, yet the Spartans were victors. This is what discipline will do. A little later in 479 B.C. in another decisive battle fought near Plataea, the Greeks again were victorious. Of Persia's 260,000 soldiers, only 3,000 returned to their homes, while the Greeks lost only 154 men out of their 100,000. Their overwhelming victory was largely the result of the discipline and valor of the Spartan heavy infantry.

The Spartans trained and disciplined themselves so carefully for their country's sake. How much more should we Christians be willing for training for Christ's sake. The fact is that much of our trouble after sanctification is because we were not properly disciplined when young. We would not be so apt to withdraw our surrender when the going becomes difficult if we knew disciplining of the body. Because we were never disciplined and always have gone the easy way, we begin to say, "A surrendered heart and life is wonderful but is it really necessary? There surely must be an easier way." But for the disciple of Christ there is no easier way than the way of the Cross. We are continually choosing either to follow the way of the Cross or to go back. And God's Word says, "If any man draw back, my soul shall have no pleasure in him" (Heb. 10:38 A.V.).

Many think that after the crisis of sanctification everything is settled, and all that is needed is to fold one's hands and wait for heaven, so to speak. But this is not so. The Lord does not make a new character for us at the crisis of sanctification, for we are to make our own character. Yet He does deal with our disposition to have our own way and brings it to an end so that the Spirit and the Blood cleanse the heart. He also gives us a new disposition. However, we ourselves must continually put off many habits, carried over into the new life, which neither glorify God nor belong to the new man. Every habit that is off-color and off-size must be put away. One day God may say to put off a habit which He may never have said anything about before, but now He does not want it in our lives any longer. The next day or week He may point out another habit, not wrong in itself but something we are better off without. We are to put off progressively these old habits related to the old man, lest life again turn to self-pleasing.

So many confuse the old man and the flesh (human nature). They are not the same. When God speaks of His relationship to the old man, it is always of a conclusive fact: "Ye *are* dead"; "the body of sin might be *destroyed*"; "we *died* with Christ"; we *were* buried therefore with him." But nowhere in Scripture does it say that the flesh is dead. God does not kill the flesh. (Nor are many of us looking for the flesh in us to die— for when the flesh is dead, that is the end of the body until the resurrection day.) The flesh *must* be deposed as the ruling agent and then kept in the place of crucifixion. Essentially, there is nothing wrong with the flesh except when it rules and lives for itself. God condemns sin in the flesh. "They that are of Christ Jesus have crucified the flesh with the passions and the lusts thereof" (Gal. 5:24). The flesh is crucified in the sense that its dominion is ended and its place of rulership given to the Spirit. The Lord does not want to "de-flesh" or dehumanize us. What He wants is to get us cleansed from sin and then returned to His right order (where the spirit dominates and the body is a willing servant).

Because while the flesh was ruling it accumulated many garments or habits, these must now be put off. We are like resurrected Lazarus, who was once all wrapped up in grave clothes. Having raised him up, Jesus said, "Loose him and let him go." We too must put off habits related to the old man—grave clothes which do not fit us any more. This is the way of the Cross, the way which Jesus himself walked. The Spirit led Him and He obeyed the Spirit in all things. He is not asking anything of us that He did not do himself. He had flesh like every other man, for the Word speaks of Him "in the days of his flesh." The only difference was that His flesh was not sinful; it was not ruling. Only sinful flesh (human nature as a ruling agent) must be rejected and deposed. Only when the flesh rules is it sinful. When the Spirit rules, the flesh is pure and right, an expression in the visible of the personal spirit.

A very homely illustration may help us in this matter of putting off old habits. A man was once given to eating far more than he needed, more than enough for two ordinary men. Thus he was decidedly overweight. He generally ate his meals at the same restaurant; the waitresses knew him well. Because when he ordered his dinner he always used to say, "I want three steaks, extra potatoes, and two [sometimes three] pieces of pie," he was called the three-steak man.

But one night while proceeding toward the restaurant on a different street, he was drawn to a gospel meeting through hearing a song that his mother used to sing. It was the first time in many years that he had been in such a meeting. Something moved in his heart, a tug which he had never experienced before. He listened intently to the message of salvation through Christ. More and more his heart was drawn out, and finally he was led to Christ. The three-steak man was born of the Spirit.

With a light heart he left the mission hall on his way to order his dinner. More hungry than usual (it was about two hours later than his mealtime), he ordered only one steak.

"Did I hear right?" asked the waitress. "I presume you want three steaks as usual?"

"No," he said in a firm tone, "just one, and one piece of pie." Never had he done this before. What had happened? For years and years he had been eating more than twice what he needed, but now he realized that it was wrong to eat like that. Gluttony was a sin. So he said no to his abnormal appetite, and ate just an ordinary meal. That first night he could hardly sleep. It was a terrible struggle, but he went back the next morning and ordered no more than an ordinary amount. In a week or two he was perfectly satisfied with a normal meal.

As it was with the three-steak man, so it may be with us. We may have many bad habits that need to be controlled and to which we must say no. For instance at mealtime, even though we may still seem to be hungry and every nerve in our being clamors for immediate satisfaction, we often must say no and refuse to give in to our strong desire for more. The same principle holds true for other flesh-controlled habits. They must not rule us. If we want to be disciples of Christ and remain so, we must put off many old habits, take up our cross, and follow our Lord.

Some say that we live on half of what we actually eat, and the doctor lives on the other half. I believe there is much truth in that. The most common ways of letting our body rule are our habits of eating and sleeping, and our other appetites or passions. We must do what Paul says and keep the body "under," for we are running a race and want to run so that we may attain. It is absolutely necessary that "every man that striveth in the games exerciseth self-control in all things." Those early Greek boys disciplined themselves not only in eating but in those other habits that the rest of the world indulged in. Just for the purpose of making their bodies strong to fight better or to attain a "corruptible crown," the Greeks lived clean lives. How much more should *we* discipline *our* bodies for a "crown that fadeth not away"? What a difference there would be today if *all* Christians disciplined themselves to become better soldiers for Jesus Christ.

Lord Roberts was a field marshal in the English army at the time of the Boer War. England was greatly distressed in the dark situation and asked Lord Roberts if he would lead the campaign. Quietly he said, "Yes." Thinking he surely did not understand the difficulties and the perils of the time, they began to explain the situation and then asked him again to lead the forces. Lord Roberts said not a word until they were through. Then he replied, "For twenty years I have been training for this campaign." Lord Roberts was *ready!*

How long have you been in training to be a soldier for Jesus Christ? How long have you disciplined yourself in the matters of exercise, of eating, of sleeping, of prayer life? We too are in an army. Jesus Christ, the commander-in-chief, is calling for soldiers who are willing to discipline themselves, take up the cross, and deny themselves not only that which is sinful but also those things that may be right. He is calling for those who are willing to lay aside every weight so that they might run for Him, not in self-energy (creaturely activity) but in the power of the Holy Spirit operating through their lives in the new man.

"The Son of God goes forth to war,
    A kingly crown to gain;
His blood-red banner streams afar:
    Who follows in His train?"

CHAPTER FOURTEEN

THE DAILY APPLICATION OF THE CROSS-SACRIFICE

> "King David said... Nay; but I will verily buy it *for the full price:* for I will not take that which is thine for Jehovah, nor offer a burnt offering without cost" (I Chronicles 21:24).

"WHEN Christ calls a man to himself, He bids him come and die," says Dietrich Bonhoeffer in his book *The Cost of Discipleship*. The words of Bonhoeffer, who sealed his testimony with his own blood (he was killed by Hitler), are true; and in them is contained the essence of Christian discipleship—*"come and die."*

There are three different kinds of dying, or should we say three different inroads of the Cross of Christ. Each creates a deeper fellowship with God and a greater conformity to Christ's death. As a result, even as Christ promised, God releases the very life of Christ through men in an unhindered stream of grace so that "from within... shall flow rivers of living water" (John 7:38). As we have already said before, the first kind of dying is *death to the old life* in the initial crisis

173

of justification. "If any man is in Christ, he is a new creature: the old things are passed away; behold, they are become new" (II Cor. 5:17). Thus, for the sake of Christ, the Substitute, all who repent and believe in Him are pardoned and born from above.

Later, there is *the death of the old man*—that is, the carnal mind, the "sin that dwelleth in us," the contrary principle in those who are justified but not sanctified. As the Holy Spirit reveals the self-life in all its subtle forms, we Christians discover our deep derangement and the enslavement of our nature to the things of the world. Longing and seeking for a deeper deliverance from these problems of the inner life, we learn that Christ took the sinner, as well as his sins, to the Cross. Then a crisis occurs. From then on, we reckon on the fact of the death of our old man —we reckon ourselves dead and alive—dead to the whole sordid business of self, but alive unto God and His kingdom of love. Then, in place of the old bitterness and jealousy, the envy and impatience (to say nothing of temptation plaguing us to greater sins), we can begin to bring forth the ninefold fruit of the Spirit— love, joy, peace, etc. (Gal. 5:22).

But there is a third kind of dying—*the death of the new man*. This deals neither with the sinner nor yet with his sin but rather with the "new" man, that is, with cleansed humanity and the physical body. (In this is included death to creature comforts, to security and to avoiding pain at any cost.) To maintain the decision made in the crisis of sanctification, there must be a *daily* handing over of the new man to God that He may plant it and thereby bring forth fruit. Paul calls this "always bearing about in the body the dying of Jesus, that the life also of Jesus may be manifested in our body."

The Apostolic Church knew this dying daily; therefore it produced genuine disciples, true learners of Christ. But about 300 A.D. the chill of worldliness crept into the Church and began to produce nominal Christians. When the true followers of the Master spoke against this low level of Christian living, the leaders, too wise to deny there was a higher level, offered opportunity for those who wanted to be out and out for God, to join a monastic order where they could separate themselves from the world and live only for God. Though such communities were founded by sincere men whose motive was right, yet these leaders did not solve the problem of Christian living, but merely recognized two levels. Ever since, we have wrongly had two classes of Christians.

Today, all admit that the Church at large is not what it ought to be, yet for the most part the idea is prevalent that discipleship with its demand for cross-bearing is wonderful but not necessary. And so, to be called a Christian today does not necessarily mean that one takes up his cross and follows Christ. The commonly used term *Christian* is no longer synonymous with the term *disciple* of the Lord Jesus Christ. Men who are *not* disciples of Jesus also use the term Christian. But a true Christian *must* follow the example of Christ in daily dying. One word in the Apostles' Creed that sums up Christ's whole life and sayings is the word "suffered." Even so, Jesus not only expects us His followers to have the joy of forgiveness, and divine peace and assurance of eternal life, but to follow Him in lives of sacrifice. Having been "taken" by the Cross, we are not only to live sacrificial lives but to find that the only life that satisfies is the life of sacrifice. The Spirit of Jesus dwelling within will lead us by the way of suffering and the Cross, and then from the Cross blessings of life and salvation will flow.

In the last chapter we showed that this way involves disciplining and ruling our body by the Spirit, and not allowing our body to rule us. Let us now go on to discover how this disciplined body must be used sacrificially for others. The way of the Lamb is the way of sacrifice. But how can we sacrifice? Primarily, there are two sacrifices which we can make: first, sacrificial giving; and secondly, sacrificial living. We can sacrifice what we *have*, and what we *are*.

When we sacrifice what we have, we call it sacrificial giving. Remember David at the threshing floor of Araunah? When Araunah, a yielded Jebusite, offered David oxen for the sacrifice, as well as the threshing instruments and the yokes of the oxen for wood, David refused to accept them without charge, saying, "Nay; but I will verily buy it of thee at a price; neither will I offer burnt-offerings unto Jehovah my God which cost me nothing." So, too, giving without cost is no sacrifice. To learn sacrificial giving, we must be prepared to pay the price.

In the New Testament we find three levels of Christian giving: *First*, there is *proportionate* giving, for Paul tells us to lay aside according to the degree in which God has prospered us. He does not state the amount, but no doubt expects at least what is commanded in the Old Testament (which was ten per cent plus some extras which made it fifteen per cent). The *second* level of giving is illustrated in Zacchaeus, who, when he was saved, gave half of what he had. (The fourfold restitution perhaps took the rest.) But there is still a *third* and deeper level. We find it in the case of the widow who did not have much but gave *all* that she had. This pleased Jesus so much that He called His disciples' attention to her act. Today God is looking for men who will give sacrificially. Lest in any wise we think we are giving too much, read Brenton Thoburn Hadley's "The Nail-Pierced Hands":

> Lord, when I am weary with toiling,
> And burdensome seem Thy commands,
> If my load should lead to complaining,
>   Lord, show me Thy hands,—
>   Thy nail-pierced hands,
>   Thy cross-torn hands,—
> My Saviour, show me Thy hands.
>
> Christ, if ever my footsteps should falter,
> And I be prepared for retreat,
> If desert or thorn cause lamenting,
>   Lord, show me Thy feet,—
>   Thy bleeding feet,
>   Thy nail-scarred feet,—
> My Jesus, show me Thy feet.
>
> O God, dare I show Thee
> My hands and my feet?

The true Christian life is a sacrificial life. Not only must we sacrifice what we *have*, but also what we *are*. It costs more than money. It will cost time, effort, comfort, and security. We must learn how to live in such a way that we no longer seek to save ourselves but are willing to be broken, and thereby to reveal the Christ within. There are countless ways to give of ourselves. Sacrificial living is not only sharing our funds but, as Isaiah says, drawing out of our souls to the hungry, satisfying the afflicted soul (Isaiah 58:10).

This is the way Paul lived. He said, "I die daily" (I Cor. 15:31). As we have mentioned before, the context is very plain and shows clearly that this reference is not dying to sin but actual physical death, a daily willingness to hazard his life to death. The preceding verse says, "We stand in jeopardy every hour." The following verse says, "After the manner of men I fought with beasts at Ephesus." It would require the greatest stretch of the imagination and the greatest liberty in exegesis to apply this phrase, *I die daily*, to death to sin. It does not at all refer to sin here but to Paul's willingness to sacrifice his life that others might live. Someone has said, "I once saw the trail of a bleeding hare on the snow." That describes the life of the Apostle Paul—"in deaths oft." Wherever he went, he left his blood. He never saved himself, but over and over again literally sacrificed *himself*.

Yes, friends, when we are "taken" by the Cross, we too will live sacrificial lives because we love Christ. The crisis of sanctification, including cleansing from indwelling sin and the filling with the Holy Spirit, merely gives quality to our life so that we can present it to God as a living sacrifice. The crisis of sanctification is no substitute for sacrificial living. Those who have already been made pure, holy, and acceptable are called by the mercies of God to present themselves as a living sacrifice. The crisis of sanctification is not the end but merely the means to an end in the Christian life. God saves and also sanctifies us in order that our lives will have the proper quality that can produce good fruit. Jesus said the same thing in just a little different way: "Except a grain of wheat fall into the earth and die, it abideth by itself alone; but if it die, it beareth much fruit" (John 12:24). We plant good seed, purified seed, seed with life in it. But it is planted not for purification but for reproduction. It is necessary first for us to be made pure and made holy so that our lives will have proper quality. Yet we must not stop there, but allow ourselves to be planted into a deeper experience of death so that fruit will be the result.

That great soldier of the Cross, Willis Hotchkiss, was once telling of his early life in Kenya Colony, East Africa. In those days of pioneer mission work (about 1895) missionaries had to live on native fare (even ants), for they could take along little equipment and no special food. Once he lived, so he said, for two and one half months on beans and sour milk. Another time, for weeks on end he was without the commonest of all necessities—salt. He also mentioned his fear of attacks from man-eating lions. They had other sufferings too. After giving a long account of the dangers of living there, of how many lost their lives, and of the costliness of the whole thing, he concluded by saying, "But *don't talk to me about sacrifice*. It is no sacrifice. In the face of the superlative joy of that one overwhelming experience, the joy of flashing that miracle word, Saviour, for the first time to a great tribe that had never heard it before, I can never think of these forty years in terms of sacrifice. I saw Christ and His Cross and I did this because I loved Him." Then he quoted Watt's matchless song:

> When I survey the wondrous Cross
>   On which the Prince of Glory died,
> My richest gain I count but loss,
>   And pour contempt on all my pride.
>
> Were the whole realm of nature mine,
>   That were a present far too small.
> Love so amazing, so divine,
>   *Demands my soul, my life, my all.*

"Do you like your work?" someone asked another missionary in Africa. "Like this work?" he replied; "No. My wife and I do not like dirt. We have reasonably refined sensibilities. We do not like crawling into vile huts through goat refuse. We do not like association with ignorant, filthy, brutish people. But is a man to do nothing for Christ which he does not like? God pity such a one. Liking or disliking has nothing to do with it. We have orders to *go* and we go. Love constrains us." Such is the drawing power of the Cross.

When the gospel message today leaves out the Cross, it has no chance of having its claims taken seriously. The strength of the appeal of communism lies in the call to the crucifixion of self. It copies more of the Christian principle of the Cross than present-day Christianity. The human heart instinctively recognizes the sign of the Cross as the sign of God. Self-sacrificing Communists today find their power in the principle of a cross. This power has enabled them in six years to increase the extent of the Kremlin's dictatorship from 193 million to 800 million—about 100 million per year! But theirs is a cross without Christ; therefore, though it is powerful, it has for them no lasting benefit.

A Communist's reproach of us Christians appeared in *Paix et Liberte'* and was quoted in the British *Dawn*, March, 1952:

> The Gospel is a much more powerful weapon for the renewal of society than is our Marxist philosophy; but all the same, it is we who will finally beat you. We are only a handful, and you Christians are numbered by the million; but if you remember the story of Gideon and his three hundred companions, you will understand that I am right.
>
> We Communists do not play with words. We are realists and seeing that we are determined to achieve our object, we know how to obtain the means. Of our salaries and wages, we keep only that which is strictly necessary, and we give up the rest for propaganda purposes. To this propaganda we also "consecrate" all our free time, and a part of our holidays. You, however, give only a little time and hardly any money for the spreading of the gospel of Christ.
>
> How can you believe in the supreme value of this gospel if you do not practice it, if you do not spread it, and if you sacrifice neither time nor money for it? Believe me, it is we who will win, for we believe in our Communist message, and we are ready to sacrifice everything, even our life, in order that social justice shall triumph; but you people are afraid to soil your hands.

What an indictment! What a reproach to soft, promise-seeking, cross-evading, self-centered, disobedient Christians of today!

It is humiliating for us Christians today to contemplate the fact that godless communism makes deeper claims on the person than present-day Christianity. In our orthodox emphasis on the blood, we have forgotten the Cross and its claims. We preach the blood and insist on its mention in almost every paragraph, but we do not *live* the blood. The practical application of the blood is needed, as it is referred to in Hebrews 12:4: "Ye have not yet resisted unto blood, striving against sin."

Christianity has not always been as weak and crossless as it is today. The early Methodist preachers knew what it meant to burn out for God. Their average life span for the first fifty years after Wesley's death was only thirty-two years! The saintly Samuel Rutherford said, "It is folly to think to steal to heaven with a whole skin." Luther said, "God's mark is upon everything that obeys Him. No tree bears fruit for its own use, nor eats of its own fruit. The sun does not shine to warm itself. In God's will everything gives itself." Only Satan and men under his influence seek their own. Everything that "seeks its own" closes itself to the inflow and outflow of divine love.

That pioneer warrior for Christ, C. T. Studd, knew the power that came through crucifixion of self. When almost at heaven's gate, he was urged to retire and take it easy. A friend wrote him saying in the language of his old sport, cricket, you've played good innings, not out; now it is time for you to declare, and hand the bat to a younger man; then I will see that you spend your last days in comfort." After thanking his friend most sincerely, Mr. Studd answered, "I'm the captain of a small army. The enemy is pressing on the right hand, on the left, and in front. Our hands are cleaving to our swords. What, shall I turn my back upon the enemy and leave my little force to fight alone? Never! I will die with the sword in my hand." And so he did! Incidentally, ten thousand Christians who had been raw heathen when he came to the field sixteen years before, attended a memorial service a year after his death.

We must preach Christ and His highest call with the widest and deepest application of the Cross so that the believer may be delivered from the power of sin, Satan, the world, and the flesh. We are commissioned to make not nominal Christians but disciples. Only in this way will we have the power in the Church that will not only equal but greatly surpass the claims and power of communism. This is the day of grace, and we still have the opportunity of a great revival. We would have the greatest revival the world has ever had if Christians would return to Biblical, Christ-centered, cross-bearing Christianity.

Is it too much for our Lord to expect us to leave all and take up our cross and follow Him? One look at Calvary and at Christ's thorn-crowned head, marred face, blistered hands, blood-stained feet, spear-pierced side, scourged, torn, wound-scarred body and sin-crushed heart should awaken in us such unutterable love for Him that we would count it a joy to know the fellowship of His sufferings.

Wilbur Chapman looked into the rugged face of General Booth one day and asked, "What is the secret of your power and success?" Tears came and stole down his cheek. Then brushing back the hair from his brow, furrowed through years of battles, trials, and victories, he said, "I will tell you the secret. *God has had all of me there was to have.* There have been men of greater opportunity, but from the day I caught a vision of what Jesus Christ could do, I gave all to Him." That is the spirit we need today.

> *Hast thou no scar?*
> No hidden scar on foot, or side, or hand;
> I hear thee sung as mighty in the land,
> I hear them hail thy bright ascendant star,
> Hast thou no scar?
>
> *Hast thou no wound?*
> Yet I was wounded by the archers, spent,
> Leaned Me against a tree to die; and rent
> By ravening beasts that compassed Me, I swooned;
> Hast thou no wound?
>
> *No wound? No scar?*
> Yet, as the Master shall the servant be,
> And pierced are the feet that follow Me;
> But thine are whole: *can he have followed far
> Who has no wound nor scar?*
>
> —Amy Carmichael

CHAPTER FIFTEEN

THE DAILY APPLICATION OF THE CROSS—
BROKENNESS

"The sacrifices of God are a *broken*
spirit: A *broken* and contrite heart, O
God, thou wilt not despise"
(Ps. 51:17).

THOUGH King David, the Psalmist, had sinned
grievously, yet he sought and obtained the forgiveness of his sins. "Jehovah is nigh unto them that
are of a *broken* heart, and saveth such as are of a
contrite spirit" (Ps. 34:18).

Yet forgiveness was not the end of all God's working. David now prayed to God for a deeper work of
grace:

"Behold, thou desirest truth in the inward parts;
and in the *hidden* part thou will make me to
know wisdom. Purify me with hyssop, and I
shall be clean: Wash me, and I shall be whiter
than snow. *Create in me a clean* heart, O God,
and renew a right spirit within me" (Ps. 51:
6, 7, 10).

David wanted that which is a blessed possibility for
every Christian—a clean heart (entire sanctification).

This is a definite crisis experience and not merely a matter of growth in grace. In the biographies of the saints, this experience has been testified to down through the years. Though different terminologies are used, all are in agreement regarding a definite point of time. And today, even those who may have very different ideas of sanctification, as far as the method of realization is concerned, are found together praying for the very same things—a clean heart and power in service.

But important though the crisis of entire sanctification is, it is not enough. A clean heart is not the end but only the beginning. The experience of sanctification *can* be lost, and one *can* fall from grace (Gal. 5:4). Thus, after the initial cleansing of the heart, there is a holy life to be lived. As we have been pointing out, man first needs illumination regarding the *fact* of the Cross, then a *faith experience* of the Cross, but this in turn must be followed by the *spirit* of the Cross— the lamb-like spirit of Christ. The initial knowledge of the Cross and the experience of the Cross *must* be followed by the spirit of the Cross, for the Cross is not only the gateway to our entire sanctification but also the principle of our daily life. We need to know this application of the Cross, which is best explained by one word—brokenness.

On this subject there is very little teaching. Few seem to know that even repentance is not *an act* performed but *an attitude* to be maintained in the Christian's life—an attitude called brokenness. This lack is the reason that in holiness circles so many come forward again and again. At the time of special meetings

some of the same seekers are at the altar every year.
The fact is that though we Christians be ever so holy,
our experience of sanctification may be lost if we are
unbroken. God has told us to humble ourselves, and
the only humility accepted is that of brokenness. The
only life consistent with the experience we profess is
a life of brokenness where the old retaliation is gone
forever, and where we live in utter humility, in absolute dependence on Christ and on His blessed Holy
Spirit. This is brokenness. There is an ancient Hindu
proverb which says, "We can walk on the dust forever,
and it will never answer back." The very words
humility and *human* come from the Latin word *humus,*
meaning the black earth on which we walk.

Humility is often identified with penitence and
contrition, and as a consequence, there appears no way
of humility but by keeping the soul occupied with sin.
But humility is something else and something more.
In the teachings of Jesus and also in the Epistles, humility is mentioned with no reference to sin; in fact,
humility is the very essence not of sinfulness but of
holiness. Humility is the displacement of self and the
enthronement of Christ. Humility means Christ is
all and self is nothing. It is not merely a succession of
humble acts, but the expression of a broken spirit. Thus
a spirit of humility, a spirit of brokenness means no
retaliation, no defense. For instance, notice the nature
or spirit that Christ claimed in Psalm 22:6, "I am a
worm, and no man." Thus when reviled, he reviled not
again. Though beaten, mocked, and spat upon, yet "he
opened not his mouth," for a worm *never* raises its
head and hisses at anyone—a snake *always* does. A
worm, though like a snake in its appearance, is en-

tirely different in nature. Do what you please to a worm, it never fights back.

The Apostle Paul speaks of humanity as fragile earthenware. He says we Christians are but earthen vessels with a treasure within (II Cor. 4:7–12). But why is Christ, the treasure, put in such a frail vessel? In order to reveal that the power of a Christian's life is *of God* and not of self. Every breaking of the vessel serves God's purpose to reveal the treasure within. Breaking causes gain, not loss. "Pressed on every side, . . . perplexed, . . . pursued, . . . smitten down"—all this is designed and planned not for our hurt but for our breaking, that the Son of God, concealed within, may be revealed.

A good illustration of the way that brokenness reveals the treasure within is Gideon and his broken pitchers. Each of Gideon's three hundred men was given a trumpet, a pitcher, and a torch within the pitcher. Then they separated into three groups. When they reached the outermost part of the camp, Gideon with his hundred men blew their trumpets and broke their pitchers. The rest of the "army" did likewise. It was then that the light was seen. As a result, three hundred men put to rout a hundred and thirty-five thousand of the enemy! Through three hundred, Gideon did what thirty-two thousand swords of his original army could not do.

Today we have been blowing our trumpets (preaching the gospel), but we have not been letting our frail earthen vessels be broken; consequently our preaching and testimony have not been "in power, and in the Holy Spirit, and in much assurance" (I

Thess. 1:5). We may be wholly following the indwelling Christ just as Gideon's men followed their leader, but by refusing to break and by refusing the Cross of sacrifice, we are limiting our God. Christ is not seen. To have Gideon's success, we must follow in Christ's footsteps wholly—blowing our trumpets and also breaking our pitchers. Only then will light be released to break forth and shine out unhindered.

The treasure dwelling within us is Christ. In Him there is not the slightest lack in purity or in power. In Him we too have all things. He longs not only to fill our own lives with His gracious Spirit but to overflow through us. But our hard shell of unbroken humanity holds back this flow of life. The reason that Christ is not seen very much today is that we are not broken. If therefore we expect to reveal Christ, we must break. He *must* have broken vessels. When the poor widow *broke* the seal of the little pot of oil and poured it forth, then God multiplied it to pay her debts. Mary *broke* her beautiful alabaster box (rendering it henceforth useless), but the pent-up perfume filled the house. Jesus took the five loaves and *broke* them, and the bread multiplied sufficiently to feed five thousand. Jesus allowed His precious body to be *broken* by thorns, and nails, and spear, so that His inner life might be poured out for thirsty sinners to drink. The seal of Christ's tomb was *broken* to give the world for all time the witness of Christ's resurrection. A grain of wheat is *broken up* in the earth by death. God *must* have broken vessels. Unbrokenness hides our treasure, the Lord Jesus Christ; only brokenness will reveal Him.

At the beginning of his career as a disciple of Christ, impulsive, inconsiderate Peter was certainly hard and unbroken. More than once the Lord had to reprove him. But after his experience of Pentecost, as well as after his experience of trials, sufferings, and persecutions, we find a new Peter. He had not only undergone a crisis experience, which changed the very center of his being, but even that crisis experience had been tested and tried in the furnace of trials and suffering. Peter was now a subdued and tempered soul. Because of this, Peter could be used to write letters of comfort to a severely persecuted church. For such a commission the "old" Peter would have been absolutely unqualified. A study of Peter's Epistles indicates that he had learned well and had experienced the very teachings he himself had received some years before from his Lord in the Sermon on the Mount: "Blessed are ye when men shall reproach you, and persecute you, and say all manner of evil against you falsely, for my sake. Rejoice, and be exceeding glad: for great is your reward in heaven: for so persecuted they the prophets that were before you" (Matt. 5:11, 12).

God's way of breaking us is by humiliations which try us and vex us. At each such occasion we choose either to break or to harden. In such cases, if we choose to be broken—in wealth, in self-will, in ambitions, in worldly reputations, in affections; despised of men and utterly forlorn and worthless—then the Holy Spirit will take and use us for God's glory.

We must learn this spirit of humility from the Lord Jesus Christ, even as we learned pride from the god of this world. Jesus invites us: "Learn of me; for

I am meek and lowly in heart: and ye shall find rest unto your souls" (Matt. 11:29). In this same passage we are shown how to learn this humility, for we are offered Christ's yoke. What was this yoke of His? It was His daily consecration to the will of His Father at any cost. This yoke (of the will of the Father) Jesus offers us when He says, "Take my yoke upon you." Before oxen enter the yoke with other oxen, they are first broken. Even so, before we become partners in Christ's yoke, we must first be broken; we must surrender our own will in full preference to the will of God; we must in a crisis *die out to our own way*, and then learn from Christ the way of the Holy Spirit's lordship. The yoke of Christ is easy, but "the way of the transgressor is hard."

Brokenness is the only antidote to the recurring sin problem. Confessing sins does not get at the root of the matter. Just as in weeding a garden we dig out the root as well as pull off the top of the weed, so the root of self-will must be slain in the crisis of entire sanctification. After that, it must not be allowed to revive. A definite altar experience must be followed by brokenness of spirit. This will mean no plans of our own, no money of our own, no time of our own. We are as yielded to God as we are to others. A principle which is often overlooked is this: "He that loveth not his brother whom he hath seen, cannot love God whom he hath not seen" (I John 4:20). So also, if in obedience to the Word of God we are not submitted to those over us in the Lord in our different relationships here on earth, then it is a definite indication that we are not submitted to God.

This principle of submission seems hard and unfair only to the unsanctified, to the unbroken. To those who have entered in to this daily aspect of the Cross which we call brokenness, it is the way of blessing. Some ignore the wonderful principle of submission; some resent this part of God's revelation; some even try to laugh off their responsibility. However, the Bible is unmistakably plain in its teaching on this subject. All are to submit to God. Wives are to submit to their husbands, children to parents, younger to the elder, rulers to those over them in the Lord, etc. The "broken in spirit" neither evade, nor avoid, nor rebel against the principle of submission. On the contrary, they find submission a plain and smooth path, with the light of God's Word as their Presence (as well as their direction and protection).

When we are truly broken, time is not needed to plan right reactions, for when we are touched by circumstances of this life, it is possible to react correctly and in love every time. But so often we must apologize for words spoken on the spur of the moment. This simply reveals a hasty, unbroken spirit. Someone said, "I don't mind people using me for a door mat and wiping their feet on me, but I wish they wouldn't scrape so long." Such are not words from one with a broken spirit.

To break is both God's work and ours. When He brings pressures to bear, we really have three choices: to rebel and resist; to despond; to break. When we break, Christ is revealed. It is easy to say "I surrender all" during our quiet time or in a public meeting, but to follow through and "walk out" such a decision is another thing. It is surrender and consecration in action. "I beseech you therefore, brethren, by the mercies of God, to present your bodies a living sacrifice, holy, acceptable to God, which is your spiritual service" (Rom. 12:1). Brokenness is the way of divine love, the only way of living "unto all pleasing." This is the way of real holiness and power. Such is the daily application of the Cross—brokenness.

CHAPTER SIXTEEN

THE DAILY APPLICATION OF THE CROSS—
INTERCESSION

"The Lord wondered that there was
no intercessor" (Isa. 59:16).

T HE disciples of Christ were privileged to witness
His wonderful works; in fact, it was amazement
upon amazement and wonder upon wonder as they
saw the deaf hear, the blind see, the leper cleansed,
the sick healed, and the demon-possessed delivered.
Daily their Master performed acts far above them. No
doubt time after time, especially when they were alone,
they had discussed among themselves the power He
displayed in His wonderful works. They also saw a
definite connection between His works and His prayer
life. Again and again when they noticed that early in
the morning He was missing, they would later find
Him on the hills or in a grove alone with His Father
in prayer. This caused a great desire to spring up in
their hearts to learn from Him the secret of prayer—
to be like Him in prayer.

Today, too, Jesus' example in prayer produces the
same desire in us to know the secret of a better, richer,
longer, and more alive prayer life. God has called every

Christian to be an intercessor for others, for our task is to stop the plague of sin and corruption that is in the world, and to stand between the dead and the living. Yet very few Christians are really satisfied with their prayer ministry for others.

The nation Israel was also called to intercede on the behalf of others. At times they fulfilled this ministry. For instance, in Moses' day, when a judgment was on Israel as the result of Korah's rebellion, and when Korah himself and his ringleaders were speedily judged, a plague began. But when the people complained and murmured, Moses told Aaron the remedy—intercession.

> "Take thy censer, and put fire therein from off the altar, and lay incense thereon, and carry it quickly into the congregation, and *make atonement for them*: for there is wrath gone out from Jehovah; *the plague is begun.* And Aaron took as Moses spake, and ran into the midst of the assembly; and, behold, the plague was begun among the people: and he put on the incense and made atonement for the people. And he stood between the dead and the living; *and the plague* was *stayed*" (Num. 16:46–48).

God wants watchmen that shall "never hold their peace day nor night." He wants remembrancers to "take no rest, and give Him no rest, till He establish, and till He make Jerusalem a praise in the earth" (Isa. 62:6 and 7). And so, if there is any truth of Scripture that ought to break the heart of man, it is found in the following passages where God says *He found no intercessors.* The word of the Lord came to Ezekiel saying, "I sought for a man among them, that should build

up the wall and stand in the gap before me for the
land, that I should not destroy it; but *I found none*"
(Ezek. 22:30); and "The Lord saw that there was no
man, and wondered that there was *no intercessor*"
(Isa. 59:16). (It may be that some of these prophecies
refer to the future as well as to the past, but certainly
the principle involved in them— that *God is looking for
intercessors*—remains the same.)

Earlier in this prophecy of Isaiah, the Lord God
had said to His people, "Produce your cause, . . . bring
forth your strong reasons" (Isa. 41:21). The Christian's
"strong reasons" are the promises of God. God's revealed will for His people is a walk of faith and prayer,
and His way of finding faith in His people is for them
to remind Him of His Word and of His precious promises. God, then, expects us to pray according to His
Word, remembering His promises, and reminding Him
of them. Then in *His* time He will answer according
to His Word. What a place of responsibility is ours
as intercessors! But alas, too often God cannot find
those who will take hold of His promises. We are like
Israel of old, like God's chosen people who, looking
everywhere else for help except to God, were ultimately defeated and taken captive and their city destroyed.

Intercession is far more than a seemingly satis-
factory private prayer life. It is a dreadful responsibility for a Christian to be an intercessor. This is
dramatically revealed in the following incident in the
visions of Ezekiel 9. After Judah's apostasy, as well as
her abominations, had been revealed to the prophet
Ezekiel, God instructed him in a vision to call together

the leaders of Jerusalem beside the brazen altar. There a man in white linen, with a writer's inkhorn by his side, was to go through the midst of the city and *set a mark* upon the foreheads of the men that sighed and cried because of the sin in their city. After that, those with weapons in their hands were commanded to *slay utterly* everyone who did *not* bear the mark (the mark of an intercessor), beginning at the sanctuary! While they were smiting, even Ezekiel thought this was too much—too dreadful. The Word says, "While they were smiting, and I was left, . . . I fell upon my face, and cried, and said, Ah Lord Jehovah! wilt thou destroy *all* the residue of Israel in thy pouring out of thy wrath upon Jerusalem?" (9:8). God had to use drastic means to cause His people to realize their position and responsibility as intercessors.

An intercessor, then, laments and sighs over the condition of the world. But a true intercessor does more than that—he prays with authority. God gave mankind authority on this earth in the very beginning, for Adam was told to subdue the earth and have dominion over it (Gen. 1:28). This promise of authority, though spoken to man in his unfallen state, has never been revoked. It was temporarily forfeited because of the Fall and because of sin in the world, but through regeneration (that is, the restoration of the image of God) this authority is restored to man. Therefore a Christian's main commission is to cause life—to bring about the salvation of sinners. We are to replenish the earth with living Christians. The celebrated Pascal once asked, "Why has God established prayer?" and then answered his own question: "To communicate to God's creatures the dignity of causality; to give us a touch and taste of what it is to be a creator." As God's word to Adam was "have dominion" (Gen. 1:28), so God's word to us is Matthew 28:18, 19: "All authority hath been given unto me in heaven and on earth. Go ye *therefore*, and make disciples of all the nations." Obedience to this command of Christ is possible only through proper intercession.

Man has been hunted and hounded and beaten; he is discouraged and distressed and frustrated—all because he does not understand his position of authority and does not know how to pray. In many cases he is not willing to pray. Long after the Fall, God said, "The heavens are the heavens of Jehovah; but the earth hath he given to the children of men" (Ps. 115:16). It is still God's plan that we take our proper position as sons of God and exercise the dominion that belongs to us as redeemed, regenerated people. Although "Jehovah hath established his throne in the heavens; and his kingdom ruleth over all" (Ps. 103:19), He rules over all through His people. These represent Him; they do His will; they fulfill His purposes. How does man exercise the dominion that is his? Through prayer and intercession, taken seriously. We must have a clear grasp of both our privilege and our responsibility, and besides that, a willingness to believe and to obey.

There is a difference between a prayer warrior and an intercessor. A prayer warrior has a burden; an intercessor has a purpose. A prayer warrior prays for things; an intercessor offers himself to God for the fulfillment of His purposes. Prayer warriors expect to get their prayers answered; intercessors *must* get theirs answered. Intercessors know God's will. They offer themselves. They let nothing stop them from seeing God's wonderful purposes realized. Christ is their example. He is not only Saviour, but Intercessor. He interceded at Gethsemane; He interceded all His life. As a result, the Church was born and is living to this day. Even now, Christ is interceding and looking for other intercessors.

Consider Moses and Paul, two of the great intercessors in Scripture. Moses knew both the privilege and blessing of intercession. In his time alone with Him on the mountain top, he learned much from God. After Israel's great sin, he climbed the mount to meet God again and to pray that He would forgive His people. He knew that the people deserved nothing but judgment. Yet to the people he said, "Ye have sinned a great sin: and now I will go up unto Jehovah; peradventure I shall make atonement for your sin." His intention, the secret locked in his heart, was to offer himself as an atonement; so he prayed to God, confessing Israel's sin: "Oh, this people have sinned a great sin, and have made them gods of gold. Yet now, if thou wilt forgive their sin—; and if not, *blot me, I pray thee, out of thy book* which thou hast written" (Ex. 32:31, 32). In this prayer is an unfinished sentence. Perhaps the reason was that Moses broke out in a great sob and was weeping for his people. *This* is intercession. *This* is prayer. God, of course, could not accept Moses' offer to die for his people, for only Christ could do that. But on the basis of the coming sacrifice of Calvary, God did forgive Israel in answer to Moses' prayer (Deut. 9:19; 10:10).

The Apostle Paul also knew how to intercede. He prayed much like Moses when he said, "I say the truth in Christ, I lie not, my conscience bearing witness with me in the Holy Spirit, that I have great sorrow and unceasing pain in my heart. For I could wish that I myself were anathema from Christ for my brethren's sake, my kinsmen according to the flesh" (Rom. 9:1–3). Paul, fifteen hundred years after Moses, had the spirit of Calvary. He knew how to pray. He too entered into the very spirit of Calvary. As a result Israel will be restored and saved as a nation. (This seems to be taking place in our day, for though Jews are returning to their land in unbelief, the day is coming when as a result of Paul's intercession a whole generation of Israel will again turn back to God.)

If the Church would only awaken to her responsibility of intercession, we could well evangelize the world in a short time. It is not God's plan that the world be merely evangelized ultimately. It should be evangelized in every generation. There should be a constant gospel witness in every corner of the world so that no sinner need close his eyes in death without hearing the gospel—the good news of salvation through Christ.

For the rest of this chapter there is another important aspect of the whole subject of intercession to consider—the priesthood of all believers. We evangelicals are very proud that we know *every* Christian may have *direct* contact with God. We are sure that no mediatorial priest is needed. Thus, one of the cardinal doctrines of evangelicals is "the priesthood of all believers." So assured are we of this fact that we even object to calling a minister a priest, and over and over again we declare: let him be called a prophet but not a priest. All believers are priests.

For this doctrine we have Scriptural grounds. Does not the Apostle John say, "He made us to be a kingdom, to be *priests* unto his God and Father" (Rev. 1:6)? The Apostle Peter states the same thing: "Ye are an elect race, *a royal priesthood*" (I Pet. 2:9). Likewise the writer of the Epistle to the Hebrews says, "Having . . . , brethren, boldness *to enter into the holy place* by the blood of Jesus, by the way which he dedicated for us, a new and living way, through the veil, that is to say, his flesh" (Heb. 10:19, 20). Such passages of Scripture state categorically that *every Christian is a priest*, with the unspeakable privilege of coming into the very presence of God, into the holy of holies. In olden times such a great privilege was not allowed to all. The ordinary priest could not enter into the holy of holies. This office belonged solely to the high priest, and that only once a year. But today the priesthood is *for all believers*.

This position of the priesthood of all believers is freighted with privilege, with benefits, and with blessings. Therefore it is no wonder that this doctrine has been taught in evangelical circles. However, the question comes, Has it been well taught? Do we know what this great fact, the priesthood of every believer, really involves? I am afraid not. Benefits and blessings as priests are great, but the responsibilities are even greater. Sad to say, we have magnified our privileges but minimized our responsibilities. To come to a knowledge of these priestly *responsibilities* by a careful study of the office of the priest in the Old Testament would doubtless bring a reluctance to claim the *privileges* of that priesthood. However, a Christian can *not* take the blessings without taking the responsibilities also.

Now it was not for himself that the high priest came into the holy of holies (except as a member of the nation Israel). Not for his own sake but for the people's sake he entered into this sacred place. For them he brought in the blood, sprinkled it on the mercy seat, and there made atonement. Before God he presented the blood (emblematic of the blood of Jesus Christ) in order that the living God could forgive Israel's sin because of the blood.

The universal priesthood of believers is also a New Testament doctrine. Today, the true believer priest presents the blood of Jesus Christ before the Father, both for the individual and for the lost world. He does for the lost what they will not do for themselves. He pleads the value of the shed blood of Christ for their forgiveness. He intercedes. The believer-priest then not only asks petitions of God, but supplicates. He makes intercession; he bears the burden of the sins of the unrepentant. Of course he cannot bear sins away as Christ did; only the Son of God can make atonement with His own blood. But on the basis of the blood of Christ, every Christian can come to God and make intercession. Truly we know not how to pray as we ought; but the Holy Spirit helpeth our infirmity and maketh intercession through us—all on the basis of the shed blood of Jesus Christ.

Israel's high priest bore the names of the tribes of Israel over his heart (Ex. 28:29). This was emblematic of his being moved in his heart, his bearing Israel on his heart. Such praying was not any cold "God bless Johnny and Sue; God bless Aunt and Uncle; God bless our church, etc." Real praying, today, is knowing something of the agony of the damned; it is feeling, in anticipation, the pains and pangs of those who shut God out of their lives and who refuse to repent and believe on Christ. Not many are willing to take on their hearts the members of the church (or even of their family). This would mean suffering—not the kind of suffering that can atone for sin, but the suffering that can feel the lostness of those outside of Christ.

Moreover, Israel's high priest bore the names of each tribe not only on his heart but also on his shoulder (Ex. 28:12). This refers not so much to feeling the infirmities and sins of those for whom he was interceding. His bearing them on his shoulder refers rather to bearing their burdens, doing for them what they would not do for themselves. Bearing burdens is intangible. It can hardly be explained, but everyone who has experienced it understands. How we need this strong praying today! Too much of our praying is wishful thinking and wishful sighing. We need men who will take hold of burdens and bear them—men who will open their hearts for the lost, who will allow God to bring them into travail of soul until Christ is formed in others. Only thus will we have success in this day of apostasy. Never in the history of our country has there been a time when religion, even the Christian religion, was so popular as today. Never has there been a time when professed Christianity has been so void of that moral quality which results in great ethical changes in both the church and the business world. For instance, the recent revelation of almost universal dishonesty in one of the greatest mediums for the transmission of knowledge—television—has shocked our nation. But the true believer-priest feels these things. He prays for persons, for the church, for the whole world. His praying is more than mere asking God to do something. It is supplicating and interceding and travailing for men and women until prayer is answered.

Remember, too, that in the Old Testament a priest was not allowed any possessions. He had a place to live but no inheritance of land for his tribe. God was his possession. In evangelicalism today, how many believer-priests would care to submit to this condition? With the true facts in mind, I wonder how many would be clamoring for the office of the universal priesthood of the believer. Today's believer-priests scramble (as the rest of mankind) for the world's possessions; yet this is in direct contradiction to Christ's word, "Lay not up treasure upon this earth." What a rude awakening many will have at the judgment seat of Christ when they discover that they have flatly disobeyed the direct word of Him who is Judge as well as Saviour! Were it not for the fact that believer-priests have sought first for possessions and then for the fulfillment of their office as believer-priests, the world would have been evangelized long ago.

Included in an Old Testament priest's responsibilities was the religious instruction of the people, as well as the discernment of the extent and effects of an Israelite's sin. Thus a priest had many functions. Consider his office regarding that dread disease of leprosy. It was his duty to pronounce a person clean or unclean. How many today who claim the priesthood of every believer would care for this solemn work in an age when we are superficially told *not* to judge? But if the benefits of priesthood are claimed, we ought to be accepting the responsibilities also.

Yet many of today's would-be priests are like the chief priests in the time of Christ—busy with rituals meaningless to them—ignorant of the true nature of their office. Many are unwilling to receive or obey the true light. Yet God is looking for *true* priests who, in accordance with their office, will "offer up spiritual sacrifices acceptable to God through Jesus Christ." He wants those who know how to mediate between a rebellious world and a God who is merciful and willing to pardon those who repent and believe in Jesus.

Perhaps this wonderful office of believer-priest is portrayed most graphically of all in the witness of Stephen before the Sanhedrin (a priestly group, by the way). Stephen had just revealed the rebellious course of Israel's history and had brought a charge of guilty upon all those who listened. Then, in the words of Scripture, "they cast him [Stephen] out of the city and stoned him: . . . And he kneeled down, and cried with a loud voice, Lord, *lay not this sin to their charge.* And when he had said this he fell asleep" (Acts 7: 58–60). The result? A religious rebel, Saul of Tarsus, became the Spirit-led Paul, the famed apostle to the Gentiles. This is priesthood! This is intercession! In this our day may God raise up true priests—true intercessors!

CHAPTER SEVENTEEN

THE DAILY APPLICATION OF THE CROSS—
WARFARE

> "They overcame him [the devil] be-
> cause of the blood of the Lamb, and
> because of the word of their testimony;
> and they loved not their life even
> unto death" (Rev. 12:11).

IN the previous chapter, "The Cross and Intercession," we referred briefly to this subject of warfare and the authority of the believer as one of the
missing aspects of prayer today. Because in the Church
of Jesus Christ there is a condition of great weakness
right here, very much more ought to be said on this
subject.

Prayer is *worship* (one should prepare himself
for this wonderful exercise); and prayer is *work*
(Luther used to speak of "sweat on the soul"); but
above all, *prayer is a battle*, for an enemy has usurped
the authority of the believer. Today, far too much of
our praying is on the level of plaintive pleading, or
is a kind of crutch to support sagging spirits. Someone
has said that prayer has three directions: there is
the *upward* prayer of worship, of praise, and of ado-
ration; there is the *downward* prayer of petition; but

there is also the *outward* prayer of warfare. That prayer today is largely downward and petitionary is self-evident. For instance, when a boy was once asked if he prayed every day, he replied, "No, some days I don't need anything." This may sound humorous, but in the prayer experience of so many of us, this is all too true. Surely we must reverse this condition. We Christians must learn to war in prayer!

Revelation 12:7–12 is a classic passage on Christian warfare and how to be an overcomer. No doubt it has a special application to a future time, but our present concern is with the universal, eternal principle set forth in these verses. According to verse eleven there are three conditions for exercising victory over Satan. The first and basic condition for authority is the blood. We overcome Satan *"because of the blood of the Lamb."* Personal victory over the flesh and the enemy is ours by the shed blood of Jesus Christ. We Christians have a right to claim this authority because, though we have no strength of our own nor any merits of our own, we have confidence in the finished work of our Lord and Saviour Jesus Christ, whose blood washed away our sins. Secondly, according to verse eleven, we not only have the right to exercise authority over Satan, but we must give testimony to our authority: *"They overcame him . . . because of the word of their testimony."* This is testimony directly to Satan himself. Because of our union with Christ, we have authority to speak out our command over Satan and his hosts of evil spirits. Lastly, this text of Scripture gives one more condition of power and authority. It declares that this authority is only operative in those who *"loved not their life even unto death.*" Authority is only for those who do not seek to save themselves but who, embracing the Cross, die to sin, to self, to the world, and to the devil. Thus, to have authority over Satan, it is absolutely imperative that one have the complete realization that he *is* a new creation in Christ Jesus. One must stand on the ground the death of Another, and on the utter crucifixion of the self-life. Such a one (and only such a one) walks with a sure and certain tread because the old life *has* been crucified, *has* died, *has* been buried, and *has* been left in the grave. There are no "landing strips" for the enemy to land on.

To believers who fulfill these three conditions and thus are said to be "on Calvary ground," God has given wonderful promises concerning warfare. Let us review some of these promises in Paul's letter to the Ephesians. First, in chapter 1, Paul says that God has "blessed us with *every* spiritual blessing in the heavenly places in Christ" (1:3); and again, "that ye may know. . . the exceeding greatness of his *power* to us-ward who believe" (1:18, 19). Only the blood-washed and God-kept can believe in such power. Next, the Apostle Paul explains that the power available to us is the same as the power needed and used to raise Christ from the lowest estate of man (death) and set Him at the very right hand of God in the heavenly places (vs. 19, 20). Think of it! The very same power manifested in the resurrection is available to us! That this passage in Ephesians has definite reference to victory in our battle with Satan, the enemy of our souls, is made plain, for now Paul goes on to explain that our position is *"far above* all rule, and authority, and power, and dominion, and every name that is named, not only in this world, but also in that which is to come" (vs. 21). Besides all this, the Apostle shows that we believers are joined to Christ, our Head, and therefore we are in Christ's position of power and authority over the enemy. Our exalted position is also unmistakably evident in the next chapter where Paul says that *we* believers were "raised ... up *with him* [Christ], and made ... to sit with him in the heavenly places, in Christ Jesus" (2:6).

The fact of our warfare as Christians is again set forth graphically in Ephesians 6. Here Paul admonishes the Christian soldier to be *"strong in the Lord,* and in the strength of his might," and to "put on the whole armor of God, that ye may be able to stand against the wiles of the devil." Here Paul brings in a most important distinction: "Our wrestling is *not* against flesh and blood, but against the principalities ... against the spiritual hosts of wickedness in the heavenly places." He goes on to say, "Wherefore take up the whole armor of God, that ye may be able to withstand in the evil day, and, having done all, to stand." Then the Apostle reminds us that for the child of God, there is a *girdle,* a *breastplate,* a *shield,* a *helmet,* and a *sword,* the Word of God. To conquer the enemy, the soldier of Christ *must* know the Word, know his place, know his position, and know his authority.

Next, one would expect the Apostle to give detailed instructions how to "hack" the enemy to pieces, but instead he says "with all prayer and supplication praying at all seasons in the Spirit" (vs. 18). This "all prayer" is no ordinary prayer but that outward prayer of authority over the enemy which the Apostle John referred to as "the word of their testimony" in Revelation 12:11. "All prayer" is testifying to the power and authority that is ours through faith in an experience of the blood and Cross of Christ. "All prayer" is testifying to the utter defeat of Satan on Calvary's Cross.

Too many Christians know nothing about this warfare because they are too occupied fighting their own inclinations and desires of their flesh. If they should enter the war, they would be defeated instantly. But for those who know that they have been *crucified with Christ*, that they have been *raised with Him*, that they are *united with Him*, and that they have *a place of holiness and power*, there is a battle— a great warfare. In this battle we are assured of victory all the way, even as Israel *before* crossing the Jordan to possess the land of Canaan was promised, "Every place that the sole of your foot *shall* tread upon, to you *have* I given it" (Joshua 1:3).

The enemy laughs, I am sure, to see Christians fighting each other when they ought to be united in fighting the devil. Of the war in Korea (called "police action") it is said that it was a wrong war, fought in a wrong place, with the wrong people, with the wrong weapons, at the wrong time! This is exactly what the enemy of our souls seeks to cause us to do. This explains why there is so much fighting amongst carnal people. They are using carnal weapons. God would say to us through the Apostle Paul: "We do *not* war according to the flesh (for the weapons of our warfare are not of the flesh, but mighty before God to the casting down of strongholds); casting down imaginations, and every high thing that is exalted against the knowledge of God" (II Cor. 10:3, 4, 5).

For us Christians, the battle is on. Yet so many, forgetting this or knowing little or nothing about warfare, blame people or circumstances or even themselves for their problems and defeats. Others may be to blame, but surely we must know that the enemy takes advantage of every situation that he can use against us Christians. Often he is behind people (Matt. 16:23). He works against the church collectively and individually—causing divisions, heresies, jealousies, fanaticism, ritualism, "rutualism," and a host of other isms. Though these isms are produced by men, they are surely inspired by the enemy. Thus for the Church today, the great need of the hour is to learn to discern what is flesh and what is Spirit, and to learn how to bind the enemy and loose souls to the glorious liberty of the children of God.

Amongst individuals, Satan has three favorite ways of working. One way is *through oppression*, caused chiefly by circumstances. Things go wrong; people seem impossible; accidents occur. Yet so many of these circumstances are caused by demon activity. Evil spirits know how to bring the one singled out for attack into circumstances that will result in a difficult time. As a result, the person attacked is in a state of frustration, futility, oppression, weariness or sickness and infirmity. (By the way, Satan is not personally omnipresent, though he is almost so through his myriads of fallen angels—the evil spirits and demons.)

Another favorite way of the enemy's working in individuals is what is called *obsession of the mind*. Here the enemy is not working so much in the outward circumstances but rather within, in the mind itself. The one worn out through Satan's oppressive tactics is a ready subject for invasion of the mind. Satan begins by planting his seed-thoughts in a mind and causing negative thinking about almost everything, even about the goodness and power of God. Satan has succeeded in making many think that they cannot pray, cannot believe, cannot serve God, cannot do anything right. Given a little wedge along this line, the enemy will finally come in like a flood. Progressively the condition then grows worse—worry, anxiety, and negative thinking; then nervousness, fear, an inability to control the mind; eventually even a nervous breakdown, or in some cases, serious mental derangement.

What the evil spirits want, however, is the third stage which is called *demon possession*. Here the enemy does not work so much in the circumstances nor in the mind but busies himself in gaining control of the will. Eventually such a person is under the power of an evil spirit, and, as a rule, is unable to help himself. He is possessed.

Today, the enemy's master weapon among Christians is ignorance of his devices (II Cor. 2:11). He has succeeded in causing the majority of people, even Christians, to disbelieve in the possibility of being possessed by evil spirits. These Christians contend that when Jesus walked on this earth, He accommodated himself to the prevalent opinion existing in Bible days, and therefore used existing terms, including the idea of demon possession. Some others say that in the days of Christ demon possession was common, and even is common now in foreign lands where idolatry is prevalent, but that in civilized lands this experience is certainly not present today, and surely not common. Yet how is it that we all admit many have a strange oppression, are obsessed mentally, seem unable to think logically, and have experiences similar to those described in the Scriptures? Surely today Satan is a *wily* foe (Eph. 6:11), and not the least of his wiles is causing great numbers of Christians to be ignorant of his devices. Paul the Apostle speaks of *the wiles of the devil.*

The first step, then, in loosing those who are helpless victims of demon activity is to diagnose the need. There are times when we really need to discern that many of the problems which we have attempted to solve through carnal methods have been caused by demon activity. All such problems can be solved only by exercising the authority given by Christ to each believer.

Moreover, one who is experiencing demon activity must first co-operate in admitting the source of the problem. If the source is not known, he should at least admit the possibility that it may be from the enemy. His next step could well be to testify, declare, and renounce the enemy by saying, "In Jesus' Name, I renounce the devil in all his works and all his ways; and I take back all ground and advantage that I have given him consciously or unconsciously. I put my faith in Jesus Christ as my Saviour and Deliverer, and I put the blood of Jesus Christ between me and the enemy. I yield wholly to my Lord Jesus Christ." This declaration is merely a guide, for victory is never a matter of repeating mere words from a written prayer. Victory is gained by a definite renunciation (which of course should include the same ideas as the sample declaration just given). Since dealings with Satan must be in such a way that Satan can hear and know our stand, it is important that it be audible. Satan cannot read the deeps of our minds (only God can do that), but Satan can hear all we say and also read surface things. And so, I repeat, it is important that the one attacked should say audibly, "In Jesus' Name, I take back every advantage and all ground I have ever given to the enemy." All this is simply using the authority that is every Christian's by virtue of union with Christ.

Once the problem is discerned as satanic, we ought to know how to proceed, for Jesus said, "Behold, *I have given you authority* to tread upon serpents and scorpions, and over all the power of the enemy: and nothing shall in any wise hurt you" (Luke 10:19). He also said, "These signs shall accompany them that believe: in my name shall they *cast out demons*" (Mark 16:17). Those who are helping in this work of mercy should make sure that they themselves are on Calvary ground, and then should command the enemy to leave, for Jesus said, "Whatsoever thou shalt bind on earth shall be bound in heaven; and whatsoever thou shalt loose on earth shall be loosed in heaven" (Matt. 16:19). Evil spirits *can* be bound and cast out; and they *can* be left bound.

In Mark 11:23 Jesus calls this form of prayer *saying* the word of faith: "Verily I say unto you, Whosoever shall *say* unto this mountain, Be thou taken up and cast into the sea; and shall not doubt in his heart, but shall believe that what he saith cometh to pass; he shall have it." This is neither plaintive pleading nor simply reminding God of His promises. This is *the word* of our testimony. This is *the word* of our declaration. This is the prayer of authority—the prayer of one who knows that he is a son of God, that he is joined to Christ, and that he is seated with Christ in the place of rule and authority and power, even in heavenly places. Such prayer is creative, for it "causes things to happen." God is waiting for believers to trust Him and exercise their rights, privileges, and responsibilities. "*All* things are possible *with God*" (Mark 10:27). "*All* things are possible to *him that believeth*" (Mark 9:23).

Many experiences could be cited concerning methods used in present-day cases. But rather than cite examples, it seems to us that the Holy Spirit should be free to lead in an original manner, that is, not according to any pattern from previous experiences. If given an opportunity, the wonderful, heavenly Holy Spirit will lead each case in detail.

In the first chapter of Genesis God said, "Have dominion" (Gen. 1:26–28). God's original commission to man in his unfallen state when he was pure and innocent included dominion. And even though sin and the Fall occurred, nowhere in the Scriptures do we read that God has changed His mind or revoked this dominionship and authority given to man. It is true that sin, defilement, and separation from God interrupted and temporarily caused man to be unable to exercise his original commission. Yet now, through redemption and regeneration, man is restored to the image of God and qualified again to exercise power from on high. Christ promised the disciples power after the Holy Ghost was come upon them. Through that power they were to preach the gospel; through that power they were to heal the sick; through that power they were to cast out demons; through that power they were to deliver the oppressed.

Today Satan, the usurper, has robbed us of the proper understanding of God's Word concerning these truths. As a result, we have not exercised the power that belongs to us. But once we know that God's original plan and purpose have been restored again through the Cross of Calvary, and then enter into God's program for us, we will do the very works that Jesus did, for He promised, "Verily verily, I say unto you, He that believeth on me, the works that I do shall *he* do also; and greater works than these shall *he* do; because I go unto the Father" (John 14:12).

CHAPTER EIGHTEEN

THE CROSS AND HEALING
or
THE CURSE LIFTED

"Christ *redeemed us from the curse of the law*, having become a curse for us, for it is written, Cursed is every one that hangeth on a tree" (Gal. 3:13).

THE curse of God was first pronounced in the Garden of Eden when God said unto Adam, "Because thou hast hearkened unto the voice of thy wife, and hast eaten of the tree, of which I commanded thee, saying, Thou shalt not eat of it: *cursed is the ground* for thy sake; in toil shalt thou eat of it all the days of thy life; thorns also and thistles shall it bring forth to thee" (Gen. 3:17, 18). Then there are references to the curse right to the very last chapter of the last book of the Bible, where we find these wonderful words: "There shall be *no curse any more*" (Rev. 22:3).

"The creation itself also shall be delivered from the bondage of corruption into the liberty of the glory of the children of God. For we know that *the whole creation groaneth and travaileth*

219

in pain together until now. And not only so, but ourselves also, who have the first-fruits of the Spirit, even we ourselves groan within ourselves, *waiting for* our adoption, to wit, *the redemption* of our body" (Rom. 8:21, 23).

The complete world-wide or, shall we say, universe-wide lifting of the curse will not take place until redemption's full and final consummation after the millennium. Then there will be nothing that defileth; then pain and sorrow will be gone forever; then death and crying will be no more; then stenches, thorns, and stings will all be gone, as well as all fevers, unbearable pains, and wasting disease. Instead of all this, we shall have Christ in His fullness; we shall see Him as He is; we shall begin to enjoy what our Lord has been preparing for us ever since His ascension.

Words fail us whenever we attempt to describe either the happy prospects of the saved, or the awful agony of the damned—who will have their pain, sickness, disease, weakness, and deformity forever, with no promise of alleviation of their awful sufferings. However, while the Scriptures faithfully set forth God's awful damnation and curse upon unbelievers, they also reveal for believers God's awful curse applied prophetically to Christ our Substitute, for we read: "If a man have committed a sin worthy of death, and he be put to death, and thou hang him on a tree; his body shall not remain all night upon the tree, but thou shalt surely bury him the same day; *for he that is hanged is accursed of God*" (Deut. 21:22, 23). That this is a prophetic word concerning Christ becoming a curse *for us* is made plain by the

Apostle Paul in Galatians 3:13, "Christ redeemed us from the curse of the law, *having become a curse for us;* for it is written, Cursed is every one that hangeth on a tree." Thus, for all who will put their trust in Christ, there is eternal hope.

Yet this redemption from the curse by Christ's becoming a curse *for us* is not only to be relegated to the final future consummation. Paul, in the very next verse of Galatians 3, connects our redemption from the curse with our receiving of the Holy Spirit, saying, "that upon the Gentiles might come the blessing of Abraham in Christ Jesus; that we might receive *the promise of the Spirit* through faith" (verse 14). Therefore, while we know that the fullness of our redemption (including the final, complete, creation-wide, permanent lifting of the curse from the whole creation) remains for the end time, nevertheless, wherever we apply the Cross to our present personal situations, we can by faith see the curse lifted in this present dispensation.

A clear application of the Cross to the curse is to be seen in the history of Israel just after their deliverance from the power of Pharaoh. Having crossed the Red Sea, they went three days' journey into the wilderness without water and then came to Marah. All were overjoyed to find the one thing they all wanted—water—so no doubt many drank hurriedly. But alas! The water was bitter, unpalatable, and unfit for use.

The scientific cause of the extreme bitterness or saltiness would be the continual evaporation; however, the disproportion found everywhere between the inflow, outflow, evaporation, etc., is the result of the curse. And so, the bitterness of the water to the children of Israel was really caused by the curse on all creation because of Adam's sin. The curse is also the cause of sickness and disease, for in this situation at Marah, sickness, bitterness, and disobedience are linked together (Ex. 15:25, 26). But God showed the remedy. After the drinking of Marah's bitter waters, there was much crying out against Moses, saying, "What shall we drink?" As usual, Moses cried unto the Lord, and He "showed him a tree, and he cast it into the waters, and the waters were made sweet" (Ex. 15:25).

The tree that the Lord showed to Moses was a type of the Cross. In the Old Testament the Cross is always called a tree. It is also called a tree in the Acts and in the writings of Peter and Paul. Applied to the bitter waters of Marah, *the tree lifted the curse*, and the waters were made sweet. This miracle symbolized the lifting of the curse because of Christ's having been made a curse for us by hanging on a tree. It was nothing with God that historically Calvary did not exist at the time of the miracle (c. 1491 B.C.), for He is from eternity to eternity, and the Lamb was slain from the foundation of the world. Moreover, the efficacy of Christ's atonement reaches not only backwards but also forwards, even to us who live in the dispensation after Calvary. Every mercy and blessing we receive today, as well as all blessings those who lived in the old dispensation received, comes on the ground of redemption. *They* looked forward to the Cross; *we* look backwards. Thus through

faith in the atonement, we *all* receive the blessing
God longs to bestow upon us.

In the concluding two verses of the passage in
Exodus 15, notice that the Lord connects the curse
with one of the three main results of the Fall—
namely, sickness, and thereby He applies the Cross to
our personal experiences wherever there is a real need.

At Marah, then, Moses cast the tree into the
waters, and they were made sweet.

"There he made for them a statute and an ordinance, and there he proved them; and he said,
If thou wilt diligently hearken to the voice of
Jehovah thy God, and wilt do that which is
right in his eyes, and wilt give ear to his
commandments, and keep all his statutes, *I
will put none of the diseases upon thee*, which
I have put upon the Egyptians: for I am Jehovah that healeth thee" (Exodus 15:25, 26).

The literal translation of the last part of this passage
is "I will *permit* none of the diseases upon thee which
I have *permitted* upon the Egyptians." ("That this is
the meaning of the word 'put' in this case requires
no proof to those who are acquainted with the genius
and idioms of the Hebrew language in which God is
again and again said to do what in the course of
His providence or justice He only permits to be
done"—Adam Clarke.) God never puts sickness on
anyone; but in certain cases (made plain here) *He
permits it*. God goes on to say, "I am Jehovah that
healeth thee." All healing, then, is on the basis of
the Cross; and so, if today we will apply the Cross
(and all that is included in Christ's so great redemp-

tion), we too will find that the results are the same
as in the case of the Israelites. The curse will be
lifted, our waters made sweet, and we will be healed
of our diseases—so healed that there will not be a
feeble man among us.

What then does it mean to apply the Cross to a
present situation? It means that it is not enough to
believe in the Cross in an abstract way. The Cross
has to become personal and practical. This is true,
we know, in the first crisis of our salvation; for before the Lord could justify and regenerate us, there
had to be personal repentance and faith. Even so, in
our present situations, though we find within us inner
conflict and much that just *will* not obey God, yet
if we will accept the Cross in its deepest meaning of
death to self, and death to all that is contrary to
God's will, then we will find that by His grace we
can obey God in everything (Rom. 8:1–4). This would
be fulfilling the conditions for healing given in Exodus
15:25, 26. Truly we will then be able to ask in faith for
healing or for any other promised gift.

To see exactly what God has promised in the matter of healing, it is important to give ourselves to the
study of God's Word. For instance, in Proverbs 4:20–
22, note the progression: "My son, attend unto my
words; incline thine ear unto my sayings. Let them
not depart from thine eyes; keep them in the midst
of thy heart. For they are life unto those that find
them, and health to all their flesh." Many rob themselves of blessing by spiritualizing the promises of God.
It is not possible to spiritualize this particular passage
because it says specifically that *God's Word is health*

to all their *flesh*. In these verses notice God's four-fold emphatic command to keep relying on the Word: "*Attend* unto my words; *incline thine ear* unto my sayings. *Let them not depart* from thine eyes; *keep* them in the midst of thy heart." It is not enough to read the Word once; we must meditate on it and keep the Word active in our minds and hearts. Moreover, this passage also explains why many good people are not healed—they simply have not *found* the word of healing. Even as many attend church for years without finding the word of salvation, and many Christians, justified for years, have not yet found the word of sanctification, so it is in the matter of healing. Comparatively few people have found the word of healing. Yet Proverbs 4 is saying that the Word of God is life to those that find it and health to all their *flesh*. It is absolutely necessary to base our faith for healing on the Word. Jesus said, "My words are spirit and they are life."

When Christ was here in the days of His flesh, He healed *all* who needed healing, *all* that came to Him, and *all* that were brought to Him. Peter said, "Jesus. . . went about. . . healing *all* that were oppressed of the devil" (Acts 10:38). And Jesus Christ is the "same yesterday, and today, yea and for ever" (Heb. 13:8). If it was God's will to heal *all* then, we believe it is His will to heal *all* who come to Him today. He is the same and always will be the same. He has not changed. It is always God's will to heal, to save, to sanctify.

According to Isaiah 53, when Christ heals, it is on the basis of His death. There on the Cross He paid the price not for our sins only but also for our sicknesses and infirmities. Yet the prophet Isaiah may well ask again today, "Who hath believed our message? and to whom hath the arm of Jehovah been revealed?" (Isa. 53:1). Even as many who heard Jesus and saw His works when He was on earth would not believe on Him, so it is today. Many who believe He can save from sin do not believe He can save from sickness. Thus they limit Christ and preach another Christ. The true gospel is this: On the Cross Christ met *all* our needs, including the healing of sicknesses—"Surely he hath borne our griefs [Heb., our sicknesses], and carried our sorrows" (Isaiah 53:4). Verse 5 goes on to say, "He was wounded for our transgressions, he was bruised for our iniquities; the chastisement of our peace was upon him; *and with his stripes we are healed*" (Isaiah 53:5).

Just as we are *all saved* potentially because of Christ's redemption, so we are *all healed* potentially through Christ's great sacrifice on Calvary. But it remains for us to appropriate healing, as we have appropriated the forgiveness of sins and eternal life. Healing is mentioned specifically in Isaiah 53, but the words in this passage are often spiritualized. Matthew 8 quotes this passage and makes very plain that healing applies to physical sicknesses as well as spiritual: "They brought unto him many possessed with demons: and he cast out the spirits with a word, and healed *all* that were sick: that it might be fulfilled which was spoken by Isaiah the prophet, saying, *Himself took our infirmities, and bare our diseases*" (Matt. 8:16, 17).

Some say this *cannot* refer to the Cross, for Christ was not yet crucified; but we have already referred to the fact that the Lamb was slain "from the foundation of the world," and that every blessing that saints in the Old and New Testaments enjoy is on the basis of the Cross (whether healing, or salvation, or sanctification, or power for service). Christ took to the Cross our sins and also our sicknesses. On the Cross every single claim against the body (as well as against the soul) was met. There our Lord Jesus Christ lifted the curse. And so it is up to us to appropriate by faith the blessing that is ours on the basis of His so great atonement.

Upon hearing this truth proclaimed, some people object by saying, "If this were true, then a Christian would never have to die." True. Jesus himself said, "Verily, verily, I say unto you, If a man keep my word, he shall never see death" (John 8:51). To Martha He said, "Whosoever liveth and believeth on me shall never die" (John 11:26). A Christian does not die like a sinner. Death has lost its power. For the Christian, it is not death; it is life, a gateway through which he enters into a higher life. The Apostle Paul calls this experience "falling asleep." God leaves us on earth to complete our time of service and probation; but when probation is finished, He takes the Christian home to himself. He who gave us life at the first can just as easily take away our breath without a wasting disease.

Christ's death on the Cross and its application in our own experience is but the negative side of

Christ's redemption—that is, a death to *all* sin *and* sickness and selfishness. But there is also a positive side plainly set forth in Romans 5: "If, while we were enemies, we were reconciled to God through the death of his Son, *much more*, being reconciled, shall we be *saved by his life*" (Rom. 5:10). To the sinner the most important thing is *the death* of Christ (which is the basis of his justification); to the Christian the most important thing is *the life* of Christ. This is explained in Romans 8: "If the Spirit of him that raised up Jesus from the dead dwelleth in you, he that raised up Christ Jesus from the dead *shall give life also to your mortal bodies* through his Spirit that dwelleth in you" (Rom. 8:11). The Spirit of God within a Christian wants to quicken him not only spiritually but also physically, and so the Word says that He quickens even the mortal body. Therefore we must trust the indwelling Spirit to manifest himself not only in our hearts and spirits but also in our bodies. This quickening power of the Holy Spirit will supersede the claims of sickness or infirmity.

Because of the law of gravity, a man's hand naturally hangs down; but within us is a law, the law of vitality, that can take precedence over the law of gravity. Through the law of vitality a man can raise his hand upward and hold it toward heaven. Similarly, the natural tendency of the human body is toward sickness. But it is possible to introduce a new law, "the law of the Spirit of life in Christ Jesus," which is able to make us free from the law of sin and of death.

We believe, therefore, that it is God's will to heal. Healing, however, is only a small part of what we have in the atonement. Christ met our every need on the Cross. Every claim that stood against us was met there in His body as He was crucified as our Substitute and Representative. To supply in a positive way all the power we need (not only to get well but to remain well in body as well as in soul and in spirit), we also have within us the quickening power of Christ's own blessed Spirit through union with our risen Lord. God longs to bestow this great blessing in times of sickness.

To help us still more in the receiving of this blessing of healing, God has condescended to our limited capacity of receiving spiritual truth and instituted the ordinance of anointing with oil for healing. Let us study in detail the ordinance of this anointing with oil. God says, "Is any among you suffering? let him pray" (James 5:14). This does not refer to sickness but either to chastening of some kind or to persecution. The provision then is prayer, either prayer that we learn our lesson quickly or prayer that we may receive grace to bear persecution and suffering. But the next verse sets forth the provision in case of sickness:

"Is anyone among you *sick?* let him call for the elders of the church: and let them pray over him, anointing him with oil in the name of the Lord: and the prayer of faith shall save him that is sick, and the Lord shall raise him up; and if he have committed sins, it shall be forgiven him. Confess therefore your sins one to another, and pray one for another, that ye may be healed.

The supplication of a righteous man availeth
much in its working" (James 5:14–16).

To help us lay hold of healing, God has given us
something to do—call for the elders, for in this way
we can act our faith. God has also given us something we can see—oil. This is not the first time that
God gave a material sign (anointing with oil) to indicate a spiritual blessing. He did the very same to
the Old Testament believers in the case of circum-
cision and of the different offerings, etc.; in the New
Covenant we have the sacraments of Baptism and the
Lord's Supper. Thus God meets us on the level of
our present experience. Because we are comprised of
material elements, as well as spiritual, He uses material elements as a sign of invisible, spiritual elements.

The anointing with oil is freighted with deep
meaning. As with most symbols it has a twofold sig-
nificance—manward and Godward. On the manward
side, oil is a symbol of consecration; on the Godward
side, oil is a symbol of the Holy Spirit. You will
remember that when the tabernacle and the temple
were completed, each part (whether the altar, the
furniture, the vessels, or the tabernacle itself) was
anointed with oil to signify that these were dedicated
to God—set apart for holy use. Even so, on the manward side, the anointing of oil indicates that the sick
one is to dedicate himself entirely to God as expressed
in Romans 12:1, "I beseech you, therefore, brethren,
by the mercies of God, to present your bodies a living sacrifice, holy, acceptable to God, which is your
spiritual service." We are to yield ourselves to God
unconditionally. Then God manifests himself. When

all sin is confessed and abandoned and washed away in the precious cleansing blood, and when we are fully surrendered to God, God's hand is stretched out to meet our hand of faith with the great gift of healing. This is the Godward side—the Spirit of Jesus Christ himself coming upon the Christian to perform the needed work of healing. When there is a proper meeting of God's supply and man's faith, healing is always the result.

Notice that the sick one is to call for the elders of the church. This is an expression of the sick one's faith. As they anoint with oil in obedience to God's Word, God honors the faith both of the elders and the sick one. Then, when this is done, according to the Word God will raise him up. What a wonderful provision for sickness—all because of Calvary! How it must grieve God's heart that in a time of sickness so few take advantage of it!

Let us then put our trust in God's Word, for God will not fail to fulfill the promises He has given us himself—such as: "I am Jehovah that healeth thee" (Exodus 15:26); "With his stripes we are healed" (Isa. 53:5); "Himself took our infirmities and bare our diseases" (Matt. 8:17); "Who forgiveth all thine iniquities; Who healeth all thy diseases" (Ps. 103:3). Man is prone to invent other ways, but God's way is the best way—placing our faith in Him who in His death has met our every need.

CHAPTER NINETEEN

THE CROSS AND HEALING (2)
or
"I AM JEHOVAH THAT HEALETH THEE"

> "O Jehovah my God, I cried unto
> thee, and thou hast healed me"
> (Psalm 30:2).

I AM Jehovah that healeth thee" is a precious
word, showing us not only that God is able to
heal and does heal, but also that *our God is a healing God*—that is, it is His very nature to heal. Yet
today, though the Scriptures are filled with many
promises of healing for God's children, there seems
to be an organized resistance to the truth of divine
healing. Though there are individuals and whole
groups of people who agree to believe God's Word, yet
more often, perhaps, whole groups disbelieve and explain away the promises of God. It was so in Christ's
day. Thus the Gospels record collective faith and unbelief (as well as individual faith and unbelief) and also
the result of each. For instance, the men of Gennesaret
"besought [Jesus] that they might only touch the
border of his garment: and as many as touched were
made whole" (Matthew 14:36). But in Nazareth
"he could... do *no* mighty work, save that he laid

his hands upon a few sick folk, and healed them. And he marvelled *because of their unbelief*" (Mark 6:5, 6).

Let us repeat some of the blessed promises of healing for the body which we have already considered in greater detail in the previous chapter.

"Who forgiveth all thine iniquities; Who *healeth all* thy diseases" (Psalm 103:3). "My son, attend to my words; incline thine ear unto my sayings. Let them not depart from thine eyes; keep them in the midst of thy heart. For *they are life* unto those that find them, *and health* to *all* their flesh" (Proverbs 4:20– 22). "Surely *he hath borne our griefs* [Heb., *sicknesses*], and carried our sorrows; ... But he was wounded for our transgressions, he was bruised for our iniquities; the chastisement of our peace was upon him; and with his stripes *we are healed*" (Isaiah 53:4, 5). "Himself took our infirmities, and *bare our diseases*" (Matthew 8:17). *"The words* that I have spoken unto you are spirit, and *are life*" (John 6:63). "To this end was the Son of God manifested, that he might destroy the works of the devil" (I John 3:8). "Is any among you sick? let him call for the elders of the church; and let them pray over him, anointing him with oil in the name of the Lord: and the prayer of faith shall save him that is sick, and *the Lord shall raise him up*; and if he have committed sins, it shall be forgiven him" (James 5:14, 15).

As has been stated already, it is God's nature to heal, so that we do not have to change God's mind by much praying; rather we must by faith get into

the right relationship with Him, and thus receive the
healing grace that is always proceeding from Him
to all who are in the right condition to receive it.
Much of our praying is on the level of pleading—
of trying to convince an unwilling God to do what
we think ought to be done. But that is all wrong.
God has made some very plain promises which He
always keeps. If we will but believe, we will receive.
It is up to us to return to obedience and the proper
application of the Cross to our inward life, so that
what blessing our Father longs to give we may receive. We are not able to do so if unbelief or disobedience or any other sin is allowed to get between
us and God. The sun, for instance, is continually
giving out its rays of blessing; but if we let something obscure the sun's rays, we shall soon experience
both coldness and darkness. So it is with the blessing
flowing from God.

That many Christians do not get healed is very
true, even as it is also true that many sinners do not
get saved. But yet a Christian who does not get
through to God for healing no more disproves the
fact of healing than does the sinner who remains
unsaved disprove the fact of salvation. Our unbelief
(or shall I say our unwillingness to believe) limits
the work that Christ longs to perform in us. Our
bodies are temples of the Holy Spirit, and He longs
to cleanse the temple from sickness, as well as the
soul from sin.

But healing of a weakened body, though a privilege for every believer, is not a necessity for salvation. To understand this, recall that the Fall

resulted in a threefold loss for man: first and most important of the three, he lost the image of God (heart holiness); second, his mind became impaired; third, his body became weakened. Ultimately, those who are in Christ will be restored fully, but at present a Christian can be saved without full restoration—that is, he can be saved and still have an impaired mind and a weakened body. But notice that he can *not* be saved without a restoration of his first loss—heart holiness, for a heart change is a moral issue and most essential. Thus, to be a child of God, his sins *must be forgiven*, and his spirit and soul *must be cleansed* by Christ's blood while he is on earth.

But the Word of God adds that *it is possible* (though not a necessity) for man's *mind* to be awakened, enlightened, and renewed here and now so that he may "prove what is the good and acceptable and perfect will of God" (Rom. 12:2). Like the restoration of the mind is the restoration of a weakened *body*. Though a man can *not* go to heaven with an impure heart, he *may* go to heaven with an impaired mind and a sick body. However, since God has promised and provided so much for both the mind and the body, why should we be satisfied with so little? Most of us live far below our privileges. For the redeemed soul, God has blessings and gifts that go far beyond the initial crisis of justification. Through the reading and rereading of His promises, we can and ought to become "strong to apprehend with all the saints what is the breadth and length and height and depth, and to know the love of Christ

which passeth knowledge, that [we] may be filled
unto all the fulness of God" (Eph. 3:18, 19).

Consider the example of the woman with the issue
of blood. She had been sick for twelve years, had
spent all she had in trying to get well but "was nothing bettered but rather grew worse." Then she
heard of the Lord and of what He was able to do.
In her heart she believed: "If I do but touch his
garment, I shall be made whole." Then one day
Jesus came by, and she had her first opportunity to
touch Him. With all the strength that her weakened
condition afforded, she pressed through the crowd to
"touch the border of his garment." *Immediately she
was healed* (Matt. 9:20–22; Luke 8:43–48). Jesus,
knowing at once that power had gone out from Him,
asked, "Who touched me?" Admitting it was she,
the woman gave the reason for her touch of faith
and then testified that she had been healed instantly.
Jesus replied, "Daughter, thy faith hath made thee
whole; go in peace."

At that time Jesus was surrounded by souls who
were blind to the possibilities of grace that this sick
woman saw. All enjoyed the blessing of Christ's
nearness (and other privileges that came from close
fellowship with Christ). All of them often witnessed
His healing acts. But she alone *experienced* the healing power of His presence, for by faith she knew
"if I but touch Him, even the border of His garment,
I *shall* be made whole." Today the Lord is longing
for others to touch Him with this hand of faith, yes,
touch no more than the border of His garment and
thereby receive virtue (power) and His healing, de-

livering, and sanctifying grace. He is more than enough to meet the needs not only of soul and spirit but also of the body. Christ is the source of unlimited power.

Now Scripture precept as well as example seems to teach that there is both elementary and advanced faith. The faith needed to obtain the forgiveness of sins and eternal life is comparatively elementary, and is only the first step into the Christian life. Next, a saved man is faced with a new crisis—full surrender and faith in God for sanctification—which is more difficult than that which is necessary for justification. But it seems that faith for healing is still more difficult, especially at a time when the Church as a whole is so reluctant to accept the teaching of the Scriptures in this matter. One who seeks healing must almost be a trail blazer, fighting his or her way through the crowd of those who do not believe that it is God's will today to heal the sick. It is not easy to take the step of faith for healing under these circumstances. Yet whenever the conditions are fulfilled, healing is lifted out of the realm of the impossible and made a blessed reality.

It would be good, now, to consider one by one seven conditions for healing. First and most important is *a clean heart*. In I John 3:21 we read, "Beloved, if our heart condemn us not, we have boldness toward God; and whatsoever we ask we receive of him, because we keep his commandments and do the things that are pleasing in his sight." Unless we have a clean heart, we will never have the boldness to step out in faith for healing. Because a doubleminded man is unstable in *all* his ways, there is an absolute necessity of full yielding to Christ and of positive faith in His blood to cleanse from all sin. For this reason, the act of healing must usually be preceded by much teaching, and the ministry of healing must include not only instruction and encouragement to receive Christ's supply but the preparation of heart for this act of faith. The first step toward healing, therefore, is heart-searching with its consequent cleansing. (Cleansing always follows when sin is confessed and abandoned, and faith in the blood of Christ is exercised.)

Secondly, we need to encourage faith by *feeding on God's Word*. We ought to read and reread the words of God about healing and then feed on them literally, for as we allow the Word about healing to be planted in our minds and hearts, it creates faith. Here are four such passages to strengthen our faith:

> "I say unto you, All things whatsoever ye pray and ask for, believe that ye receive them, and ye shall have them" (Mark 11:24). "Jesus said unto him, If thou canst! All things are possible to him that believeth" (Mark 9:23). "This is the boldness which we have toward him, that, if we ask anything according to his will, he heareth us: and if we know that he heareth us whatsoever we ask, we know that we have the petitions we have asked of him" (I John 5:14, 15). "Call unto me, and I will answer thee, and will show thee great things, and difficult, which thou knowest not" (Jer. 33:3. See also Rom. 10:17).

People often give premature declarations of faith which result in nothing but embarrassment. To avoid this and to let faith come to maturity, we must feed on God's Word until we are fully assured that what God has promised He is not only able to perform but *will* perform. Remember at Jericho how the Israelites under Joshua's leadership demonstrated that they believed God's promise by walking around Jericho's walls six days, and then on the seventh day, seven more times. But it was not until the seventh time around on the seventh day that faith reached such a level that they could declare the word of faith.

> "At the seventh time, when the priests blew the trumpets, Joshua said unto the people, *Shout;* for Jehovah hath given you the city. So the people shouted, . . . with a great shout, and the wall fell down flat, so that the people went up into the city" (Josh. 6:16, 20).

Thirdly, another condition for healing is *definiteness in prayer*. For instance, the blind beggar at Jericho, on hearing that Jesus was passing by, began to cry for mercy. He made such a disturbance that those around him felt that they had to rebuke him, and they did. But he cried louder than ever, "Jesus, thou Son of David, have mercy on me." Then Jesus sent word to have him brought to Him, and when he came near, He asked him, "What wilt thou that I should do unto thee?" He answered, "Lord, that I may receive my sight." (From this account we know that it is not enough to cry for mercy. Jesus is not satisfied with a general plea but looks for a specific request.) Jesus replied, "Receive thy sight; thy faith hath made thee whole. And immediately he received his sight, and followed him, glorifying God: and all the people, when they saw it, gave praise unto God" (Luke 18:35–43).

When we seek God for healing, we must be definite. This is no time for general prayer; we should state our particular need. Moreover, it must also be settled in our mind that it is God's will to heal, so that after we have made the petition, we do not add the words, *"if* it be Thy will." God says, *"This is the boldness* which we have toward him, that, if we ask anything *according to his will,* he heareth us: and if we know that he heareth us whatsoever we ask, we know that we have the petitions which we have asked of him" (I John 5:14, 15). We should first find out the will of God and then ask accordingly. Several Scriptures make it perfectly clear to us that it is God's will to heal. We would do well to reread Scripture passages on healing, for because of sectarian prejudices, many minds are closed to the teaching of healing.

Fourthly, after we are definite in our prayer, we must be just as *definite in our expectation from God.* Some people once went to church to pray for rain and afterwards were taunted by an unbeliever with, "If you had really believed that God would answer, you would have taken your umbrellas along."

There are, then, two classes of unbelievers: those who manifestly do not believe God will keep His promises, and those who profess but do not actually believe. The lame beggar of Acts 3 was so impressed with Peter and John and the faith they radiated that he expected to receive something from them. Peter said,

"Silver and gold have I none; but what I have, that I give thee. In the name of Jesus Christ of Nazareth, walk. And he [Peter] took him by the right hand and raised him up: and immediately his feet and his ankle-bones received strength. And leaping up, he stood, and began to walk; and he entered with them into the temple, walking and leaping, and praising God."

Fifthly, it is not enough to be definite in our request; we must be just as *definite in accepting* the answer to our prayer and in acting upon that answer. Solomon says, "For everything there is a season, and a time for every purpose under heaven" (Eccles. 3:1). So it is with healing. There is a time to ask, and there is a time to receive. At Ai, Joshua was disheartened at his defeat and fell on his face before God in prayer, but God had to say to him, "Get thee up; wherefore art thou fallen upon thy face?" (Josh. 7:10). This was a time for action and not prayer, even though there is a time for prayer.

We seldom come to faith in an instant of time. There seem to be three stages of faith: the labor of faith, the fight of faith, and the rest of faith (Heb. 4:10, 11; I Tim. 6:12). First, there may need to be some *labor of faith,* a continuing to pray until we have assurance. This is not easy, but finally after we have "prayed through," we receive assurance of the answer. Then comes the *fight of faith.* The devil will do everything he possibly can to cause us to leave our position of faith. For this reason Paul told Timothy to fight the good fight of the faith. If we stand our ground against the devil's lies and our own misgivings, sooner or later we shall enter into the third and final stage of faith—the *rest of faith*—or full-grown faith where one has ceased from his own works and is relying fully on God to do what He has promised. At this stage of faith one looks for encouragement to God alone, not to an improved condition nor to the experiences of others.

Sixthly, for healing of the body we need to *stand our ground*. The devil may come a thousand times and tell us, "That's not so! God does not mean what He says! God doesn't mean that word for you anyway!" Or, if we have been definitely healed past all argument, the devil will say, "Oh yes, you *were* healed, but you are no longer healed. Don't you see that the disease has returned?" Through a failure to stand, many have lost the blessing of healing. Thus we must be prepared to be tested and rest ourselves upon the Word of God, for God will never fail.

Seventhly, we must be willing to *act our faith*. James says, "As the body apart from the spirit is dead, even so faith apart from works is dead" (James 2:26). Jesus told the man with the withered hand, "Stretch forth thy hand. And he stretched it forth; and it was restored whole, as the other" (Matt. 12: 13). God will always give us ample opportunity to act our faith, and here we must not fail.

Finally, if we have fulfilled all these conditions for healing, then we will be ready to do as God commands us in James 5:14, 15: to call for the elders, to let them pray over us and anoint us with oil in the name of the Lord. After obedience to this word, we can rest in the assurance that *God has done the work*, regardless of symptoms or circumstances.

From this time forth, every thought and act about our condition must be positive, based upon the sure and unfailing promises of God.

Many ask, "Should means be used (such as doctors, medicines, hospitals, etc.)?" Some believe it is wrong to use means because this would be either a lack of faith or an entire denial of the Lord. Now the Bible does not say, "Call the doctor when you are sick." God says, "Call for the elders" (James 5: 14, 15). But yet it does not say that we should *not* call the doctor. And so, the first thing to do is seek God's direct help and be open to any leading the Lord may give. He knows our hearts and the quality of our faith, and He will lead. Sickness, as well as sin, we believe, is from the devil. Sickness came in through the Fall, so in order to eliminate it, any God-given means is legitimate. We should do anything the Lord leads us to do. Many of our diseases are the result of wrong habits of hygiene (lack of rest, improper food, insufficient exercise), and therefore it may be necessary to consult one who has the proper training and experience and who is qualified to give competent advice. Thus the Lord may lead us to consult a doctor or to take medicine. Doctors are doing much to remove sickness and we should thank God for them, especially for the many Christian doctors who so unselfishly give their time to fight sickness and disease wherever it is found. Yet we must be consistent here, for *if* we say that sickness comes from God, *why* should we try to remove it through medical treatment? *If* it is from God, it should be endured. The truth is that sickness is not from God but from the devil. Sin and sickness both came through the Fall at the devil's instigation, and we should not allow the devil's work to continue in the body, but by all means try to get rid of it. In any case, remember that doctors can treat, but only God can heal. Direct healing without the use of any means does give God more glory. If only we will believe, this path is open to each one of us.

In seeking to be healed, we should begin with prayer and end with praise. In Philippians 4:6, 7 we read, "In nothing be anxious, but in everything by prayer and supplication *with thanksgiving*, let your requests be made known unto God. And the peace of God, which passeth all understanding, shall guard your hearts and your thoughts in Christ Jesus."

In the matter of faith, Abraham, the father of all them who believe, is a good example for us. In Romans 4 note Abraham's four steps of faith, showing us exactly how *we* can let *our* faith grow.

"In hope he believed against hope, to the end that he might become a father of many nations, according to that which had been spoken, So shall thy seed be. And without being weakened in faith, he (1) considered his own body now as good as dead (he being about a hundred years old), and the deadness of Sarah's womb; yet, (2) looking unto the promise of God, (3) he wavered not through unbelief, but (4) waxed strong through faith, giving glory to God, and being fully assured that what he had promised, he was able also to perform" (Rom. 4:18–21).

(1) When Abraham took inventory of his and Sarah's natural resources, the results were not encouraging;

yet they did not weaken his faith. Likewise, we too in case of sickness must not deny nor minimize, but admit our condition; and (2) as Abraham turned his eyes from this hopeless condition to the promises of God, so we must look to God's Word of promise. (3) Abraham's faith grew strong because he wavered not—that is, he did not look back and forth. Abraham had done much wavering in his earlier days, but now he had learned his lesson. He now believed and for many years kept on believing God's word before he saw its fulfillment. Even so, we too must not waver by looking away from our sickness to a promise of God and then back again to the sickness. Such wavering weakens faith. Too often when we first look at the Word of God, then at what others say, and our own condition and symptoms, we fail to recognize that God's promises are more sure than our symptoms. All these things which cause us to waver in unbelief must be confessed and cleansed away in the blood of Christ.

(4) The result of Abraham's "wavering not" was that he "waxed strong through faith, giving glory to God." Keeping his eyes fixed on the promise, he became fully assured "that what he had promised, he was able also to perform," even though it was absolutely impossible from a natural point of view. If like Abraham we keep our eyes on the Word of God—knowing that the Word is backed up by the very character of God—we too will have a faith that can expect and receive. We, too, like Abraham, will have cause to give glory to God in praise and thanksgiving. We will thank God for His gift of healing, and will continue day by day to praise Him for His wonderful goodness to us.

CHAPTER TWENTY

REDEMPTION AND ITS CLAIMS

> "Redeemed with . . . the blood of
> Christ" (I Pet. 1:18, 19). "I have re-
> deemed thee; I have called thee by thy
> name, thou art mine" (Isa. 43:1).

GOD acted out His wonderful salvation in the details of Israel's exodus from Egypt the night of
the fourteenth of Nisan, c. 1491 B.C. We are justified
in believing this because when John the Baptist saw
Jesus coming to him after His baptism and His forty
days in the wilderness, John said, "Behold, the
[paschal] lamb of God, that taketh away the sin of
the world" (John 1:29). Truly the slain lamb that
Moses wrote about was a type of Christ, our Passover Lamb, who "hath been sacrificed" (I Cor. 5:7).
Let us study this favorite story of Israel's deliverance
from Egypt (Exodus 12, 13), considering first one
very well-known factor—*redemption by blood.*

At the time of the Exodus, Israel was in bondage
to Egypt. They had not always been in bondage, but
after a long time of sojourning there (about 215
years), there had arisen "a new king over Egypt,
who knew not Joseph." Afraid of the Israelites be-

cause of their increased number and wealth, this king took away Israel's possessions and then forced the people "to serve with rigour" in absolute bondage.

Israel's slavery to Egypt is a good picture of man's slavery to sin, for all men, the Bible says, are sold under sin (Rom. 7:14). Like Israel's bondage, sin often begins as a tiny and insignificant thing but very soon becomes master. We need to realize therefore that sin is an awful thing; sin is a cruel enslavement. Jesus said in John 8:34, "Verily, verily, I say unto you, *every one* that committeth sin is the bondservant of sin"—a slave of sin. When full-grown, sin brings forth death. Thank God that both in Bible days and in our own generation, faithful men of God have preached about sin, its dangers, and its remedy.

Today men are slaves to sinful habits that do not belong in their lives. They have tried hard to get rid of these habits, yet their trying always failed, for they knew not how to get free. But there is a way out of bondage to sin, even as God provided a way out for Israel from bondage to Pharaoh. By themselves, the Israelites would have failed to get out of bondage; knowing this, God had considered them already and chosen a deliverer. (God always works through men and is looking for men today—men whom He can trust, men who will obey Him, men whom He can use.) For eighty years God had been preparing His chosen man for the hour. At first Moses, God's chosen vessel, had not been ready to accept his commission, but at length he had yielded to God's will. At exactly the right time, God sent this deliverer to Pharaoh, king of Egypt, to declare, "Thus saith Jehovah, Let my people go." To this, Pharaoh replied, "No." Then you remember the judgments that God began to send. First, the rivers became blood; then came the plagues of frogs, of lice, of flies, of murrain, of boils, of hail, and of locusts; later, there was a thick darkness that could be felt. After each plague Moses went before Pharaoh, beseeching him to let the people go. Pharaoh refused. Seven times he said to God, "I *will* not." After the seventh time God said, "Thou *canst* not."

Finally, God forewarned the people of the next judgment—the death of the first-born in every single household in Egypt. It is interesting to notice that though some of the plagues were selective, the death of the first-born (a type of the wages of sin) was to come upon every household—alike in Egypt and in Israel. In the very same way God says, *"Death* passed upon *all* men for that *all* had sinned." Man's redemption is not selective because it is needed by all.

Though every first-born in Egypt had to die, God gave Moses a remedy which, if applied, would bring safety to the first-born in every Israelitish house. For God promised, "This month shall be unto you the beginning of months: ... In the tenth day of this month they [Israel] shall take to them every man a lamb, ... a lamb for a household: ... Your lamb shall be without blemish, ... and ye shall keep it until the fourteenth day of the same month" (vs. 2–6). Israel was to take a lamb with no blemish and keep it for two weeks. On the tenth day it was set apart and thoroughly tested for blemishes until the fourteenth day.

All this was a perfect picture of the true Lamb of God (Christ) who was absolutely without blemish. As we carefully follow through the last days of His earthly life, we note that He too was "set apart"—separated for burial by Mary's anointing on the tenth day of the month Nisan in 30 A.D. The morning of the next day He rode into Jerusalem on a donkey, and there later was wickedly treated—betrayed, spat upon, beaten with rods, mocked, mistreated, and had His beard plucked out. He was sent from Annas to Caiaphas, then to Pilate and Herod, and finally back again to Pilate. All these things they did to Him, but yet the Scriptures say "He opened not his mouth." Though reviled, He reviled not again. In the very beginning of His ministry He was without blemish; at the end of His life He was without blemish. Thank God for this. If it were not so, we would have no hope, for He who was to die for sinners *had* to be perfect, *had* to be without sin.

But that is not the whole story of redemption from Egypt. Jehovah spake, saying, *"If the household be too little for a lamb, then shall he and his neighbor next unto his house take one according to the number of the souls"* (vs. 4). A passover lamb could be more than a family needed but was never not enough for a family. Even so, the gospel of the suffering Saviour is ample provision for all needs. Let us thank God for the overabundance of grace—grace to meet every need, even the deepest sin that holds a sinner. Grace is never too little. The Apostle Paul knew that the gospel was able to meet *every* need of *any* fallen man, and so Paul declares that he was not ashamed of the gospel, and would not make apologies for it (Rom.

1:16). The gospel is the *perfect* way of salvation, providing *perfect* deliverance, and *perfect* cleansing, and makes possible a *perfect* Christian—the only kind that God will take into heaven (for we can *not* take *any sin* there). Some of us are not ready for heaven because we have not yet seen Him as perfect Saviour; but praise be to God, that for all who will receive Him, Jesus is a *perfect* Saviour—"without blemish."

Next, God said, "*Ye shall take a bunch of hyssop, and dip it in the blood that is in the basin, and strike the lintel and the two side-posts with the blood that is in the basin; and none of you shall go out of the door of his house until the morning*" (vs. 22). Take note that it was not the death of the lamb, nor the blood of the lamb that saved the Israelites from destruction. It was *the blood applied* that saved lives. That night in Egypt, the fourteenth of Nisan c. 1491 B.C., if the household merely killed a lamb, or even caught and saved the blood but did not apply it to the lintel and the side-posts, the first-born died. The head of a household could have said, "Well, I don't see any point in sprinkling blood; we've done almost all we were told to do. Why disfigure our house by blood? I just can't see it. It's too bloody for me." Yet to leave the blood unapplied meant the death of the first-born in that house. Only where the blood was applied was the first-born saved. Even so today, it is *not the death of Jesus*, the Lamb of God, that saves us; it is *not the blood of Jesus* that saves us. It is only the blood *applied* to the doorposts of hearts that saves sinners.

It is interesting that the blood was applied with hyssop. In ancient times hyssop was used for cleansing and medicinal purposes. It was as common as a weed—so common that someone said you could put out your hand anywhere in Egypt and touch hyssop. It grew plentifully everywhere. Surely, then, hyssop is a type of faith and of the word of faith which is "nigh thee, in thy mouth, and in thy heart" (Rom. 10:8). It is not enough to know that Christ shed His blood. That blood must be applied to the doorposts of our hearts by faith. We need to have faith in the Person and sacrificial work of the Lord Jesus Christ.

What a night that must have been in Egypt! In the stillness, the first-born in every single household died—in the houses of all the physicians and magicians of Egypt, in every priest's house, in Pharaoh's house. Doubtless there were cries from many who were weeping over their dead. Everywhere in Egypt the same thing happened.

> "At midnight, ... Jehovah smote all the first-born in the land of Egypt, from the first-born of Pharaoh that sat on his throne unto the first-born of the captive that was in the dungeon; and all the first-born of cattle. And Pharaoh rose up in the night, he, and all his servants, and all the Egyptians; and there was a great cry in Egypt; for there was not a house where there was not one dead" (Exodus 12:29, 30).

How different it was in Israel! Not one died—not one! The text seems to indicate that every single one was safe. Of course under the blood every one would be safe, but the question comes to mind, "Was every first-born in his house?" We do not know for sure what problems they had with their children in those days, but I have an idea that there may have been wayward children then too. Perhaps some were wilful and when told about the way of deliverance made excuses, as some today who say, "Oh, but I promised my friend that I would go down to the game tonight"; or, "We have a game of cards started"; or, "I was going to the dance tonight." I have an idea that there were many interruptions that night in Egypt, but I am sure of one thing— that particular night mothers and fathers made certain their first-born was in the house. Perhaps some were prayed in and others were dragged in! If the son was not at home, I think the father went out and somehow managed to get him inside the door of his own house.

If today we would only get earnest about this matter of our unsaved parents, children, loved ones, and friends—as earnest as each Israelitish father and mother that night—then all of them will be under the blood. But we are careless and not in earnest about these things. One person after another dies, and as the coffin goes down into that hole in the earth, we stand by and weep because of lost opportunities to witness, to serve, to help, to encourage. We know we are too late. Yet if we get in earnest and disturbed enough about our ease and procrastination, we are going to see souls saved. I am not thinking of parents' responsibility only, but of the Church's responsibility as well. One pastor used to go to the dances and taverns on Saturday night and look for people from his church and Sunday school. How the congregation hated him, saying, "He has no business doing that; his business is preaching!" But his most important business was looking for his sheep, the flock he had been entrusted with. Seeking lost sheep *was* his business.

So far in this chapter we have considered only the subject of redemption by the blood of the Lamb. This is very important, yet far too many of those who see Christ as Redeemer and who know they are saved from sin's penalty, stop right there and fail to go on. However, to know forgiveness of sins and justification by faith is just the beginning, just the entrance into the light. We must go on. Redemption from the hand of Pharaoh was not the end which God had in view for Israel.

And so, as we read on in Exodus 12 and 13, we will discover other important factors generally overlooked. In these passages, there are twice as many words of instruction regarding what to do with *the body* of the lamb as with *the blood* of the lamb. Where is this needed emphasis today on what to do with the body? We emphasize getting people saved (and not very well saved at that), yet Exodus gives twice as many verses on other factors of full redemption. For instance, it mentions partaking of the lamb (12:8–10); eating unleavened bread with the lamb (12:8, 15); departing in haste because of urgency (12:11); and the blood claiming all it cleanses (13:2). Let us now seek to understand what lessons God is teaching us through these details.

Israel was given very minute directions *how* to partake of the lamb: *"Eat the flesh . . . roast with fire"* (vs. 8). For a sinner, the most important thing is to be justified, to be forgiven on the basis of the shed blood; but for a Christian, the most important thing is to partake of the Lamb, to eat of the Lamb, to be strengthened by the Lamb and thus enabled to live a holy life. Having been saved by the blood, we need to be strengthened by Christ's life. We Christians today are to eat the lamb—roasted with *the fire of God's judgment.* Christ was wounded and bruised, for the stroke due us came on Him, "By *his stripes* we are healed"; by *His death* we are saved. It is a *crucified* Christ we are to know, even as Paul declared he intended to preach only Jesus Christ *and Him crucified* (I Cor. 2:2).

Concerning partaking of the lamb, Israel was also instructed, *"Eat not of it raw, nor boiled at all with water, but roast with fire"* (vs. 9). Far too many people throughout the world see Christ as just a teacher, a prophet, a leader, a founder of a religion, a speaker of good words and one with a high standard of ethics. This would be eating the lamb "raw." This is failing to see Jesus as God's Lamb. Nor must we eat the lamb boiled with water. We must not water down the gospel. Not at all. Some of us are afraid that the gospel usually presented today is "sodden in water." It is not the gospel of Jesus Christ nor the gospel of the Apostle Paul.

Men thin out the gospel. They water it down by believing that though the gospel can get people into heaven, it cannot change lives completely. We must always sin every day in thought, word, and deed, they say.

But the Bible does not say that. It tells us that heaven is a holy place for holy people, and that the blood of Jesus Christ was shed for sinners. Yet unless we have more than just the forgiveness of our sins, we *will be* sinning in thought, word, and deed. Today it is a limited gospel that is preached and not the gospel of the Book. It is a limited Christ and not the Christ of the Book. It is a limited Spirit and not the Spirit who comes to give power for inward victory and for service. Thank God, the true gospel is still in the Book so that anyone who wants to find out exactly what God says, and will do it, will be lifted up into that wonderful life of peace, purity, and power.

We are further instructed to eat of the lamb "*roast with fire; its head with its legs and with the inwards thereof*" (vs. 9). All the parts of the lamb are to be eaten. Though we need the blood of our Passover Lamb for our sins, nevertheless, for strength in our thinking, for our daily walk, and for our whole inner life, we must partake of the whole Lamb. Jesus himself said, "My flesh is meat indeed, and my blood is drink indeed. He that eateth my flesh and drinketh my blood abideth in me" (John 6:55, 56). At the Fall, perhaps more damage was done to our head (our thinking) than to any other part of us. "Every imagination of the thoughts of his heart was only evil continually" (Gen. 6:5). Therefore we need our thinking crucified at Golgotha (the place of the skull). Next, our daily walk is needy, and so we must partake of the lamb's legs. Finally, for the whole hidden and secret life we need Christ. We need Him manifested in our thinking, our walk, and our whole inner life. He wants to be manifest in us; He wants us to be partakers of His divine nature. Let us eat all the lamb. Let us partake of the life of Christ.

A second important lesson in this passage is this: "Eat the flesh... *with*... *unleavened bread*" (12: 8). Along with the lamb they were to eat unleavened bread. Leaven in the Word of God usually stands for corruption—for sin. So God is telling us here that after experiencing the benefit of the blood of the Lamb, and after partaking of the person of Christ, we are to live a holy life.

In the instructions for celebrating the feast of unleavened bread each year, the Lord declared,

> "Seven days shall ye eat *un*leavened bread; even the first day ye shall *put away leaven* out of your houses: ... Seven days shall there be *no leaven* found in your houses: for whosoever eateth that which is leavened, that soul shall be cut off from the congregation of Israel, whether he be a sojourner, or one that is born in the land. Ye shall eat *nothing* leavened; in all your habitations shall ye eat *un*leavened bread" (Ex. 12:15, 19, 20).

For seven days they were to eat *un*leavened bread. Seven, a complete number, speaks of a life of holiness. God expects us to partake of Christ in holiness. We are to be a holy people. "We... should serve him without fear, *in holiness* and righteousness before him all our days" (Luke 1:74, 75).

But there is more. Redemption with blood and partaking of the lamb is for a purpose. The Israelites were told: "*Thus shall ye eat: with your loins girded, your shoes on your feet, and your staff in your hand; and ye shall eat it in haste: it is Jehovah's passover"* (Ex. 12:11). After the lamb had been slain and the blood had been put on the doorposts, they did not have much time left for eating the lamb, for they were to leave Egypt at once. Thus they were not to recline leisurely at the table. A crisis had arisen, and on the basis of that crisis they had to be prepared for immediate action. What God was really saying was this: "Here is an emergency. I want you in the land. I want you to begin to be what you ought to be, to begin to be a blessing to Me, to begin to bless the world." But what if one of the Israelites of that day had said, "Well, I think it's all right to leave. We ought to leave, and we surely thank God that Moses came to set us free, but I can't possibly get ready that fast. And besides, I've got more things to take with me than Moses thinks I need." Surely no one spoke like that. No one thought like that. Why? Because they had their eyes open to the real conditions. They were living in a state of emergency.

Friends, ever since the real slain Lamb, Jesus Christ the Son of God, died on Calvary's cross, God himself has declared an emergency: "Get your shoes on your feet; have your staff in hand; eat in haste. Go into all the world and preach the gospel to the whole creation." In the first generation after this great commission, the Christians obeyed (without the equipment we have today which we think are so necessary). They preached the gospel to every creature under heaven, recognizing that the proclamation of Christ, the slain Lamb, was an emergency affair.

As a result, at that time *every* nation was told the gospel, for the Word declares it came to Colosse even as it "was preached in *all* creation under heaven" (Col. 1:6, 23).

Today, conditions still call for emergency measures. It is as if you saw someone reading a newspaper inside his burning home who knew not that his house was on fire. What would you do if he continued reading, even after you had called him to come out? You would drag him out, would you not? In the same way, since Calvary there has been for Christians a state of emergency so that instead of struggling for normalcy, every thing in life is to be evaluated in connection with what is most important. However, the most important thing in the world is not getting a new car, not security, not an income, but obedience to Jesus' last command: "Go . . . into all the world and preach the gospel to the whole creation." Therefore, all Christians *must* live under emergency measures.

The last phrase to consider in these two chapters from Exodus is *"the first-born . . . is mine"* (Ex. 13:2). Again God was not thinking of security nor of safety but of service. On the night of the first Passover *all* the first-born who had been redeemed from death by blood were brought into a new relationship to God. His unmistakable call to them was, "You are Mine—My absolute possession." Later at Sinai, after the golden calf episode, the special privilege and responsibility of the first-born passed to the Levites, for when Moses asked, "Who is on the Lord's side?" the entire tribe of Levi stepped forward and were chosen as

God's special representatives. Some years later, before the Levites entered the Promised Land, they were told, "There will be a tribal possession for your brothers and their families, but not for you Levites. You have no possession in the land, for God is your possession."

Since Christians get *no inheritance on earth*, their roots are not to go down into the earth. He did *not* say, *"It is better* that you do not have treasures on this earth," for He was talking to disciples. To them He said exactly the same as had been said to the Levites (using different words, of course). He did not actually say to His disciples, "You shall not have a tribal possession in the land, for God is your possession." No, He simply said, "Lay not up *for yourselves* treasures upon the earth, where moth and rust consume, and where thieves break through and steal" (Matt. 6:19). This is a definite command: "Do *not* lay up treasures on this earth." Why? The moth and rust corrupt and consume the things you try to save, but nothing will consume or touch treasure laid up in heaven.

Many Christians are always saving things for "rainy" days. However, we believe God will take care of the rainy days for all who have given their money to Him. Our possessions are in heaven, and certainly we can not lay up treasure on earth and in heaven at the same time. If we give ourselves for the purpose for which we have been saved—to evangelize the world— God will be our possession. The Apostle whom Jesus loved said in his Epistle: "Love *not* the world, neither the things that are in the world. If any man love the world, the love of the Father is not in him." The

Apostle John was not thinking about gross, coarse sinfulness; he was just thinking about "this order of things." We are *not* to set our affection on these things; we are *not* to love them, *nor* gather them. Jesus flatly forbids laying up treasure on earth.

Friends, right now in many places in our country it takes ten thousand church members to produce one missionary and keep him on the field. Something is absolutely wrong. Christ's command to preach the gospel to the whole creation has been kept only once, and that by the apostles and the Christians of that generation. Since then, generation after generation have gone to their graves not knowing of God's saving love, not knowing that the blood has been shed, not knowing anything about the Lamb. Why? We have been laying up treasures on the earth. We have been living for self, not only in a sinful and gross way, but perhaps in a refined way.

Some years ago a pastor friend of mine had in his congregation a widow with two sons. The elder was a fine young man, but the younger was wayward, willful, and a burden and grief to his mother. Usually when the younger son had done some wicked thing, his brother got him out of trouble and brought him back home. One day, however, the younger son packed his belongings and left home altogether. Hearing this, the pastor went to visit the widowed mother, but as he was about to knock, he first glanced through the glass in the door and for a while stood watching. Then, without going in, he turned and went to the field where the older brother was ploughing, and quietly remarked, "I hear your brother has left home."

"Yes, he has," said the older brother, rather grumpily.

"Well, what are you going to do about it?"

"Nothing! He's made his bed, and he's going to lie in it. I've gotten him out of trouble many times, and this is the end."

"Well, you know what he will do, don't you? Wouldn't it be better for him at home?" remarked the pastor.

"I suppose so, but I'm not going to go after him any more. I'm through!"

Then the pastor made a suggestion: "Let me plough while you go to the kitchen door and peek through the glass. Then come back and tell me what you saw."

So they parted. Before long the older brother was back and began to quit work for the day.

"Have you changed your mind?" asked the pastor.

"Well," he said slowly and thoughtfully, "nothing in my brother changed me, but one look at my mother's face has made a big difference! To see my mother weeping and praying for my brother even while she was working was just too much for me."

If we Christians really saw our Lord's face, if we saw Him weeping over the world as He wept over Jerusalem, maybe we would have a change of mind about evangelizing the world. We would ask Him, "Lord, what can *I* do? If only You show me what can be done, all I have and all I am is at your disposal." Once we have really seen Jesus' face, we will not lay up treasure on earth or disobey the commission to take the gospel to the whole creation.

So few Christians recognize the total, unconditional claims of Christ—His absolute ownership. So few believe God's words, "Except ye forsake *all* that ye have, ye cannot be my disciple." If the truth from Exodus 13:2, "the first-born is mine," were believed and accepted, what a reviving work of God there would be! Possibly then we would not even need missionaries. One convert in a foreign land would witness to another, and that one to yet another. Finally the gospel would get to the border of a country where everybody would be bilingual. Then it would jump the borders from one country to the other, and before we knew it, the gospel would be over all the world. Perhaps that was God's original plan. But the Church is so far from obedience to God's ways that we have to use another method—foreign missionaries.

In His well-organized plan of evangelizing the world, God has a place for every child of His. Are we redeemed by blood? Then we are not in the class of the ordinary Israelite but of the first-born. We are a Levite and not our own; we belong to God; we are under His absolute possession and control and are not to have possessions on earth. We are "bought with a price"—body, soul and spirit—that we may fulfill our Redeemer's commands. His Blood *claims* all that it *cleanses*.

CHAPTER TWENTY-ONE

"I SOUGHT FOR A MAN"

> "I sought for a man among them
> that should build up the wall, and
> stand in the gap before me for the
> land, that I should not destroy it; but
> *I found none*" (Ezekiel 22:30).

IN these pathetic words spoken by God to the prophet
Ezekiel, it is evident that there was great need for
men who in word and example would step forward
and stem the tide of sin—men who would bring
the people back to God and thus avert impending
judgment. God was saying, "If just *one* man really
meant business and stood in the gap, the need of the
hour would be met." God was looking for men, but
found none . . . n-o-n-e!

God is looking for men today also. Is He finding
them? To any man with strong feeling, missionary
statistics bring shame. As we hear the figures repeated
again and again, we have to bow our heads in
shame. Where are the men? the strong men? the
gifted men? the trained men? the wealthy men?
Too many of them are living for themselves.
Their prayers may be long, their testimonies

may be frequent, and they may even preach; but if they do not obey Christ, they have no right to consider themselves Christians. They are going in the wrong direction. Regardless of their testimony, if they are not obeying Jesus Christ, they are lost. A Christian is a pilgrim, a sojourner, and a stranger upon this earth. Any person who lets his roots go down into this earth is giving testimony to the world that he is earth-bound, and that he has no regard for the Word of God which says, "Set your mind on the things that are above, *not* on the things that are upon the earth" (Col. 3:2).

One day in prayer time in a missionary headquarters, little Sharon thanked God for the "aunties" going to the foreign field (the children called the women aunties and the men uncles). "But dear Jesus, won't you please send out some uncles, too, to help them do the job?" We thank God for the faithful women who are bearing burdens men ought to bear, and doing work men ought to do. God is blessing women and using them; souls are being saved, and God's kingdom is advancing. But God is still looking for men to take the torch and go forth with the unsearchable riches of Christ.

Many young men who at one time had a call to serve God on the mission field have lost themselves in secular work. They are tithing and occasionally praying for missionaries, but too often their giving and praying are but token gifts, designed to keep them from being altogether condemned.

Moreover, many leaders are afraid to give young men the proper challenge, merely saying to them,

"Well, the Lord will lead. If He wants you on the foreign field, He will show you." Our advice should rather be, "God wants you on the foreign field. If He does not, He will make it very clear to you." Keith Falconer, that great missionary to Arabia, said: "While vast continents still lie shrouded in midnight darkness, and hundreds of millions still suffer the horrors of heathenism and Islam, the burden of proof rests upon you to show that the circumstances in which God has placed you were meant by Him to keep you out of the foreign field."

A pastor was once testifying about his call into the ministry. He had been working in a plant where ball bearings were manufactured. When he shared with others the fact that the Lord had called him to the ministry, someone said, "I think you are making a mistake; God needs Christian men in business too. God needs you here in this plant." But his answer had been, "If God had considered ball bearings necessary to life, I believe He would have caused them to grow on bushes. As far as I am concerned, God has called me to preach the gospel, and that is what I am going to do." That is the spirit we like to see. That is what we like to hear.

We make no excuses for insisting that every man accept the missionary challenge and live for missions. Men are not obeying the call, and many who start well "flunk out" after a few months. So many men at Bible schools, seminaries, and missionary training centers do not "carry through" their initial call as consistently as women. They apply for training, then at the last moment change their minds and go into business or decide that the homeland needs more pastors.

Sometimes we are told that God does not want every Christian on the mission field because He wants Christians to be in business too. Maybe He does want them in business, but He wants every single Christian in His missionary program. Missions is not to be accepted as a side issue but as a Christian's real purpose for living, the real passion of his heart and soul. How long are we going to let the heathen perish "without hope" because we ourselves have not been willing to obey Christ's call?

A look into any Bible school student body will quickly show how often the women outnumber the men and the strongest men are conspicuous by their absence. Some missionary training programs attract more men than the ordinary Bible schools, but even then the proportion of men is altogether too small. I suppose that it has been this way since Christ gave His great commission. The Apostle Paul stated the very same thing a few years later when he wrote to the Corinthians that it is the foolish, the weak, the base, the despised, and *"the things that are not"* whom God uses in His plan to save men from the wrath to come. If the wise, the noble, the strong will not respond, He will accomplish His purpose without them.

A few years ago, upon the completion of a summer itinerary of special meetings in different parts of the country, we arrived home about the time the new students were arriving. Soon I was asking the staff about the arrival of new students. The reply was, "They are here, including three with physical handicaps—

one in a wheel chair!" Later, I began to consider these things. Jesus Christ, the Ruler of the universe, has called every believer to leave all and follow Him. How could it be then that the strongest, the best qualified, and the most talented were so often indifferent to His claims, while the handicapped (some in one way and others in another) were presenting themselves? My heart cried out, "Lord, how long shall the strong, the rich, the gifted turn a deaf ear to Thy call?"

Of course we do thank God for all handicapped ones who say yes to Jesus. They are doing outstanding work and are possessed of a devotion to Jesus Christ that is more than enough to make up for any physical lack. We have seen those with great handicaps healed, blessed, baptized and filled with the Spirit, and sent out to do a magnificent job on the foreign field. I think of one, a woman about forty years old, who had been almost afraid of her own shadow and unable to give a testimony in her church. At one time she was so needy physically that she had a difficult time carrying on a comparatively easy job. But she was healed, responded to Christ's call, and went to Africa. There she courageously faced difficult situations, received God's blessing in her own soul, and knew the anointing with power from on high. She is now doing an outstanding work for God on the foreign field, living alone in native villages, sleeping in native houses, and busy telling about Jesus Christ the Saviour. Another woman at the age of sixty went to the foreign field for Christ's sake. After serving with great success on one field for ten years, at the age of seventy she was transferred to a different field. Her health and strength and success is a constant amazement to her mission.

This is a time of emergency. Yet year after year we see the women, the old, the weak offering themselves for service, while in many cases the strong choose to live for self and the world. (Perhaps the men are offering themselves as prayer partners for women missionaries!) Again let us hear what Jesus says: "Whosoever he be of you that renounceth not *all that he hath*, he *cannot* be my disciple" (Luke 14:33).

Some Christians do admit Christ's claims to total ownership and step forward in response to His call. However, too frequently if one of unusual ability chooses to go with the gospel to the ends of the earth, then friends, relatives, and often even pastors and church workers say, "It's a pity; he could have gone far in this world, but now he will be wasting his life in some jungle or other out-of-the way corner of the world."

Do Christian high school graduates with straight "A" grades go in flocks to Bible schools? Or do they more often choose to go to college because they are too intelligent to spend their time merely studying God's Word, and theology, and related subjects? The world has its pattern concerning training brilliant minds. But, like thoughtless sheep, are we Christians to follow the world? Surely the devil knows that by scholarships he can subtly entice and sidetrack many first rate minds. Earnest Christians who begin to follow worldly wisdom soon lose their vision of God's great commission. Undoubtedly, for some young people, college training may be indicated by God's Spirit. But we are convinced that for further education a Christian student should choose as the first course of study the Book of books and related subjects, thus giving clear testimony to what he considers most important.

In the light of the world's great need at the present
time, we do not apologize for saying that every Christian who is young and healthy ought to prepare for
missionary service with the intention of going to the
foreign field. Then, if it is *not* God's will to go, God
will lead him definitely into business or Christian work
in this country. Certainly the first intention of every
Christian young person should be to go rather than
to stay. Though we thank God for all the young people
who have stepped out and come to training schools to
prepare for special service as God's ambassadors, the
number is pitifully small.

Does all this mean that every Christian must pack
up and move to a foreign field? No, it does *not* mean
that, yet it does mean that every Christian must be
one hundred per cent for missions. Every Christian is
in full-time service. But though God will surely call
some in the homeland to work hard and to earn money
to support his missionary program, even they are
not to become earthly minded. God may make it
very plain that we are supposed to be in business or
else work in a factory or on a farm. In that case we
should live simply and sacrificially, keeping only what
is absolutely necessary for daily living, and giving
the rest of our earnings to make possible the fulfillment of Christ's command to preach the gospel to
the whole creation. Many people already in business
could well support a greatly multiplied missionary
army if they would only accept their full responsibility. They are called to stay behind and to support,
to pray, and to give. This does not mean only ten
per cent or fifteen per cent or twenty-five per cent
giving; it means one hundred per cent giving—that

is, everything above the bare necessities of life. This is their full-time service. A Christian who is not living and working for the spread of the gospel is like a prodigal son, estranged from that which is closest to the heavenly Father's heart.

Our country has only seven per cent of the world's population, yet ninety-three per cent of our theological students remain in this country. This proportion ought to be reversed, for according to population distribution, it would be more reasonable for the seven per cent to stay at home and the remaining ninety-three per cent to occupy the foreign fields. If such were the case, many heathen would be saved, and the work at home would not suffer but flourish as never before. Much of the latent power of the so-called Christian laymen would be revealed and utilized for the glory of God. The Scriptures declare, "There is that scattereth and increaseth yet more; and there is that withholdeth more than is meet, but it tendeth only to want" (Prov. 11:24). This law of the kingdom and of nature calls upon us to scatter men and women through the world with the gospel.

How tragic that only about two per cent of the world's population is vitally Christian! In 1935 the entire missionary army numbered about 35,000. In a few years it dropped to about 27,000 of which about 5,000 were inactive (either because of sickness, furlough, or other reasons). Today the number has increased again, but it is pitifully small compared to the number of Christians at home and the great need on the foreign field. As a Church we need to be ashamed of this miserable showing in these most revealing statistics.

Every foreign land we hear from says, "Send us workers, for we are understaffed." When I was in Liberia at a beautiful mission station which cost practically nothing to build (made out of mud blocks which were plastered and painted), some Africans came from about forty miles. The mission leader reported their story to us, saying, "These three Africans walked here as a delegation seeking workers. The chief said that if only some missionaries would come to his village, he would build a house, a church, a clinic, give land, set up a nice compound, and do everything that was needed. He wanted to know if someone could come." But what could the mission leader and his wife tell them? Neither they nor the two other missionaries on that station could go, for they already had more than they could do. One of them, almost single-handed, was taking care of over three hundred lepers (while in one leprosarium in the U.S.A. there is almost one worker for each leper).

Not long ago a missionary speaker was telling at great length of a doctor who was a top man at college and possessed many varied and outstanding characteristics. He went as a missionary to India where he was living sacrificially at a salary of only $300 a month. This no doubt was a real sacrifice, for some doctors live only to lay up treasures on earth. Yet another medical missionary, less known, but also talented and gifted, who was present at that very meeting, said later that $53 a month personal allowance was sufficient for him and his family, provided that an additional $25 to $30 came in for general expenses! (This is in Africa where the cost of living is considerably higher than in India!) Not only did he state that he was willing to accept such a meager allowance, even though he was qualified to earn a large salary, but under these conditions he was headed back for his second term and praising God for the privilege. The Bible standard is this: "Having food and raiment we ought therewith to be content" (I Tim. 6:8).

This is the hour of reappraisal. Many may come to the conclusion that though they have considered themselves Christians for years, they are as lost as are the Hottentots (perhaps more so, for the heathen may never have heard the gospel nor had a chance). The Bible calls some people "twice dead."

> "Woe unto them! for they went in the way of Cain, and ran riotously in the error of Balaam *for hire* .... These are they who are hidden rocks in your love-feasts when they feast with you, *shepherds that* without fear *feed themselves;* clouds without water, carried along by winds; autumn trees without fruit, *twice dead,* plucked up by the roots" (Jude 11, 12).

I thank God for everyone who is disturbed and whose false faith is destroyed. If he will repent and come to Jesus, God will give him *living faith,* and the result will be *living obedience.* "Be ye doers of the word, and not hearers only, *deluding* your own selves" (James 1:22).

Someone once talked about sacrifice to C. T. Studd, the founder of the Worldwide Evangelization Crusade. "Sacrifice? I don't know anything about sacrifice," he said, "It's no sacrifice to be here." Although he was fifty-two years of age and a sick man, he went out to Africa. He had already served God as a missionary in

China and India, but now he left his wife for eighteen years and saw her only once—for two weeks. He lived, served God, and died in the heart of Africa. C. T. Studd poured out his life for God. I talked to the workers right on the field where he had worked, and they said he would sometimes put up his arm and say, "Look at this arm. Why, it's nothing but a stick. If persecution came here, I'd just crumble. Oh, I wish I were strong so that I could suffer for Christ. I can't suffer much any more."

Someone sent C. T. Studd a letter telling him to come home because he had been on the field long enough. "Give up your leadership and hand over your bat to a younger man. Then come home and we'll see that you are secure and comfortable for the rest of your life."

"Comfort," he snorted; "I hate that word." So he sent word back, "No, with the enemy facing me on the right hand, on the left, and before me, the sword cleaves to my hand. I'm the captain of a small band. I can't leave them now." And he didn't. He died there.

Today God is looking for soldiers like that—both those who will stay home and work hard and support the program, and also young people who will go to the ends of the earth to preach the gospel, not looking for a soft life but "snorting" when they hear the word comfort.

May God help us to read again Christ's commission in the Bible and then be honest before Him and before men. If we are not one hundred per cent for missions in all that we do and earn, then let us fall on our faces before Him in repentance, in confession, and in consecration to Christ and to that which is His heart's desire—the evangelization of the world.

In view of God's so great salvation and the total lordship of Christ, a decision is certainly in order. C. T. Studd's plain and simple decision form is as follows:

"To your knees, man, and to your Bible! Decide at once! Don't hedge! Time flies! Cease your insults to God; quit consulting flesh and blood. Stop your lame lying and cowardly excuses. Enlist! Here are your papers and oath of allegiance. Scratch out one side and sign the other in the presence of God and the recording angel. Mark God's endorsements underneath."

HENCEFORTH

For me	*For me*
	or
To live is Christ	Chocolate my name
To die is gain	Tepidity my temperament
I'll be a militant	A malingerer I
A man of God	A child of men
A gambler for Christ	A self-excuser
A hero	A humbug
Sign here	Sign here
- - - - - - - - - - - -	- - - - - - - - - - - -

God's promises are sure in either case

"Lo, I am with you alway" (Matt. 28:20).

"I will spew thee out of my mouth" (Rev. 3:16).

We of Bethany Fellowship fully endorse C. T. Studd's challenge.